QUESTIONS ABOUT CHRISTIANS

CHRISTIAN PIATT

with Matthew Paul Turner,
Carol Howard Merritt, Doug Pagitt and
others not afraid of impertinent questions

CHALICE
PRESS
ST. LOUIS, MISSOURI

Visit www.chalicepress.com

10 9 8 7 6 5 4 3 2 1   13 14 15 15 17 18 19 20

Print: 9780827202870   EPUB: 9780827202887   EPDF: 9780827202894

Library of Congress Cataloging in Publication data available upon request.

Contents

Contents

Contents

Introduction

Why a Book about Banned Questions?

When I was younger, I had a Bible thrown at my head during a Sunday school class for asking too many questions. Granted, I was probably even more provocative than your average adolescent, but I really did have a lot of legitimate questions about God, my faith, Jesus, and the Bible.

The message I got at the time was that church isn't the place for such questions.

Seriously? If we can't ask the tough, keep-you-awake-at-night questions within our faith communities, then what good are they?

I left organized religion behind for about ten years, until I found a place where my questions not only would be heard and tolerated, but also respected and wrestled with. Beyond that, the good people at Chalice Press have had either the nerve and/or the lack of judgment necessary to offer me a book series to help others struggling with these same questions.

In these pages you'll find some of the most provocative, challenging, or otherwise taboo questions about Christians and the Christian faith that many of us have wondered about but few have actually asked. I assembled an incredible team of respondents to offer their views on these hard questions. Their responses range from the personal to the profound, and from sarcastic to deeply touching. I'm deeply grateful for each of them, and for their commitment to sharing their hearts, minds, and experiences.

The goal of this book is not to resolve these difficult issues once and for all, but rather to open up an ongoing dialogue that allows us all to talk more openly together about what we believe and what we don't, and, perhaps more important, why we believe it.

I strongly believe that any faith worth claiming should stand up to rigorous examination, and should also be open to change over time. I hope that this collection is one step in your continuing journey as a person of faith, whatever that may look like to you.

If you enjoy this book, be sure to check out *Banned Questions about the Bible* and *Banned Questions about Jesus*, the first two books in the Banned Questions series. And if you have questions you'd like for me to consider for future editions, or if you think of a topic for another *Banned Questions* book, write me at cpiatt@christianpiatt.com and tell me about it.

Christian

Can you be LGBTQ and be a Christian? A minister? More denominations and Christian communities are welcoming LGBTQ people, as well as ordaining LGBTQ as ministers. Is this really possible?

Andrew Marin

Who is...
Andrew Marin

For over 20 years I had a pet iguana named Iggy who grew to be over 5 feet in length.

A. The answers to these questions are best described by a good friend of mine who is gay. He says, "If 'Christian' means I trust Jesus alone to bring me into right relationship with God, and if 'gay' means I experience sexual attraction and romantic feelings toward people of the same sex, then I qualify as a gay Christian. At one point I chose to be a Christian, and over a period of time, I discovered I'm gay.".

Contemporary society must start deconstructing its understanding of a gay Christian. Depending on who you ask, gay Christians are either fully acculturated LGBTQ people who have integrated their faith and sexuality, or they are oxymorons that can't actually exist. The expectation is that the correct response must land in only one of those two camps. The remaining question begs, then, what about the LGBTQ person who legitimizes his or her LGBTQ orientation and then chooses to be celibate based on a conservative theological interpretation? Can that person correctly self-identify as a gay Christian?

Many fighting this debate would suggest "no." And, denominationally, if one disagrees with "the other" regarding the various progressive and conservative interpretations of gay relationships and ordination, does that give the right to go ahead and justifiably delegitimize the realness of the other's conviction and filtration? There must be more nuance added to this conversation, even in what seems to be the most simple of questions.

Brian Ammons

Who is...
Brian Ammons

The sound of pulling napkins out of metal dispensers sends chills up my spine.

When I was ordained I'd quite visibly identified with the local LGBTQ community for years. It was understood by the community where I was serving that my experiences as someone who had stood on the other side of religious-based violence was part of the gift I brought with me to my ministry. As a Baptist, our tradition is that the ordaining body is the congregation, so the decision was made at a local level. I was fortunate to be ordained and serve a community who knew me well and partnered with me in discerning a call to vocational ministry.

Our contemporary Western understandings of sexual identity are pretty different from the time and place in which Jesus lived. I think most of the church's current debate about LGBTQ inclusion is really about our diversity of views concerning sexual identity and scriptural hermeneutics. For example, if you think about sexual identity as being mostly made up of habits or behaviors, and you look to literal interpretations of the *King James Bible*, of course you'll see the ordination of LGBTQ folks as contrary to Christian teaching. However, if you understand sexual identity as a sacred gift drawing us into being more fully human through our desire to love and be loved, and you understand Scripture as a record of a people's experience of God in a specific time and place, which still has distinct and powerful meaning for us, it's totally reasonable that you would come to a different understanding.

While I might say that most of the positions we hear articulated can stand within the broader Christian tradition, it's not to say that they are all equally appropriate. In the end, the question for me is, Which is the more Christlike stance? —and I come down on the celebration of the gift of love.

Margot Starbuck

Who is...
Margot Starbuck

I had an amazingly impressive Superball collection as a youngster.

At the heart of this question, I hear the wondering, "Can someone that the Church has historically identified as a sinner be a Christian?" The asker could be a curious LGBTQ pagan or a wondering straight Christian or a doubting LGBTQ person raised in the Church. Regardless of the faith convictions or political opinions or moral leanings of the asker, whether affirming or judgmental, the "Christian" answer is *necessarily* a resounding yes. To suggest otherwise is just nutty.

Whether queer brothers and sisters are welcome by denominational bodies to shepherd flocks as pastors is another can of worms. Faithful and intelligent academics and pastors and laypeople within the network of congregations in which I am situated, the Presbyterian Church USA, have been debating this one for years. And years. And years. Those who welcome LGBTQ folks into leadership maintain, from Scripture, that committed monogamous relationships are not condemned in the biblical texts. Those who would deny ordination to LGBTQ folks maintain, from Scripture, that sexual intimacy is only permitted within the bounds of heterosexual marriage. Among this latter group, some do ordain LGBTQ Christian leaders who have chosen celibacy.

Though the Church continues to have a difficult time navigating this one, intelligent loving faithful folks do, in fact, host each of these opinions. And while, in the midst of our differences, it's tempting to abandon relationship with the other, our calling is to practice genuine good-seeking love for one another. That is where the rubber hits the road.

Two Friars and a Fool

Who is...
Two Friars and a Fool

One of us is an ordained Spiritual Humanist,
and has only ever done secular weddings.

Not only is this possible, it's awesome! Lots of amazing people are now doing ministry openly that they've done throughout Christian history while being forced to hide who they really are. LGBTQ equality is the right side of history and is a movement of the Spirit in our age.

If you dig deep into the Bible, you can contort a half-dozen passages and claim they are referring to modern, committed, same-sex couples living out their sexual orientation as we now understand it. You're wrong, but you can make the case, and even make it sound kind of compelling. But why would you want to? Nothing in Scripture demands that we treat LGBTQ folks like less than people, less than fully made in the image of God, or any more sexually sinful than their straight neighbors. Outside of these half-dozen poor, contorted Bible passages, there is no justification whatsoever for this kind of behavior— not in ethics, nor in law, nor in the social or physical sciences. Not to mention the overwhelming witness of Scripture, which is that God is in the boundary-breaking business when it comes to love and the blessed community.

Right now, thousands of LGBTQ folks are ordained clergy, in multiple denominations, and are leading the body of Christ in worship, prayer, sacraments, and service. Many more LGBTQ people of faith are loving God and following Jesus and empowered by the Holy Spirit. Right now. You can't stop them, and why would you want to?

Scriptural reference(s):

John 13:34–35

Suggested additional sources:

- *Bulletproof Faith* by Candace Chellew-Hodge (progressive) *Out of a Far Country* by Christopher Yuan (conservative)
- A Loose Garment of Identifications by Brian Ammons (2010) http://homebrewedchristianity.com/2011/03/02/thats-too-gay-brian-ammons-banned-chapter-from-baptimergent/
- www.gaychristian.net – Gay Christian Network has a really useful booklet that helps congregations study the Scriptures on both "sides" of this issue. (I understand how even visiting the site could be a little anxiety-producing for some, but it really is a very fair, thoughtful, valuable resource. What makes GCN a particularly valuable resource to a variety of congregations is that it includes both affirming gay Christians and those who choose to practice celibacy.)
- *On Being Liked* by James Alison
- *Sex and the Single Savior* by Dale Martin
- *Jesus, the Bible, and Homosexuality: Explode the Myths, Heal the Church* by Jack Rogers
- http://twofriarsandafool.com/2010/10/lgbtq-ordination-resource
- http://twofriarsandafool.com/2009/03/not-a-sin-introduction/

Questions for further discussion/thought:

1. What is your understanding of a gay Christian?
2. Have a conversation with a theologically conservative gay Christian and a progressive gay Christian. Listen to their stories and notice the differences about how they came to formulate their understandings of labeling themselves as gay Christians.
3. How would our conversations about sexuality change if we were to focus less on questions of sexual identity and more on questions of sexual practice?
4. What would it look like to approach sex as a form of prayer?
5. What word could you put in this sentence to which the answer would be no? "Can you be _____ and be a Christian? (A discussion starter!)
6. To be a member of the Levitical priesthood, your body had to be whole and without defect, you had to be a male descendant of the

right families, and you had to fulfill a wide variety of ritual purity requirements. When Jesus died, the curtain of the Holy of Holies was torn in half, signifying the end of the Levitical priesthood and universal access to God. Whom would Jesus exclude from the priesthood today, and why?

7. Have you ever met any people, or heard of any, who chose their sexual orientation?

8. Can you think of any way that a Christian leader's sexual orientation would make a difference in how he or she prays, worships, shares in the sacraments, counsels and serves people, etc.?

Source cited:

- *Love Is an Orientation: Elevating the Conversation with the Gay Community* by Andrew Marin (Downers Grove, Ill.: InterVarsity Press, 2009)

Preachers such as Joel Osteen preach about Jesus wanting us to be rich. Where does this belief come from? Wasn't Jesus poor? Didn't he tell rich people to give everything away?

Jonathan Brooks

Who is...
Jonathan Brooks

I love glassblowing.

A. The idea that Jesus wanted us to be rich is a very popular notion. As a representative of a group of people who have been marginalized and underresourced in this country for over a century, I understand why many minorities flock to this kind of teaching. Our white counterparts seem to enjoy the teaching because it does not challenge the American idea of comfortable living, even if it is at the expense of others. I simply remind people when they ask me this question that Jesus was obviously not a fan of the rich. He didn't hate them, but he always challenged them. When the rich young ruler came to Jesus to inquire about going to heaven, Jesus let him know that his main problem was his love for things. He told him to sell everything and then come back and follow him to see if he would really do it. Sadly, that was too much to ask of him. The truth is, our mistreatment of people and selfishness has lead to the prominence of this teaching. Being rich is not a bad thing, but it can be a problem. So much so that Jesus is quoted as saying it is easier for a camel to go through the eye of a needle than for a rich person to get into heaven. OUCH!

Margot Starbuck

A. Though God did promise prosperity the Israelites as they entered the promised land, the wacky Christian extraction of this—a la Osteen—is called the "health and wealth gospel." And though health and wealth are certainly values our *culture* endorses, they're nowhere to be extolled in the life or teaching of Jesus. Rather, repeatedly, in a variety of phrasings, Jesus exhorts his followers to lose their lives, to give them away, to sacrifice themselves, to bear their crosses, which is kind of the polar opposite of health and wealth.

Given our natural human predilection toward comfort, though, it's easy enough to convince ourselves that Jesus *does* want us to be happy, healthy, and rich by our clever reading of the Bible. When Jesus says, "Do not store up for yourselves treasures on earth" (Mt. 6:19a, NIV), we *hear*, "As long as I don't have as much money as Brad Pitt and Angelina Jolie, I'm good." When Jesus says "For where your treasure is, there your heart will be also" (Mt. 6:21, NIV), we hear, "Even though my heart and mind perseverate on making more money, and buying new shoes, and eating fudge sundaes, I am totally *not* like Disney's greedy Scrooge McDuck, who runs gold coins through his four-fingered duck-hands all day long…because I don't *own* gold coins…. So, I'm probably good." And when Jesus says, "You cannot serve both God and money" (Mt. 6:24, NIV), we hear, "I *can* serve God and money" because we've been shaped more by our culture than by Christ.

Phil Jackson

Who is...
Phil Jackson

I used to drive a tractor trailer, putting gas in gas stations.

A. I grew up poor, and when you grow up fighting over chicken wings, you dream of a time when you can have enough money to buy chicken wings for the whole block. No one likes being poor in a world that advertises that you are not good enough unless you have *this* type of shoe, *this* type of car, or *this* type of house. The poor often feel left out; therefore, capitalism drives desire. When you live without, your life is defined more by what you don't have than what you do have, even though in all reality you are very wealthy in terms of community, family, and even in faith. It is not glamorous to be poor; no one is filling out applications to be poor; you feel less than human.

I believe this is the reason Christ came to preach the gospel to the poor and to set the captives free. He taught in many stories how he came to demonstrate the love of God to the "least of these." Jesus, in part, quoted a passage of scripture from the Old Testament that defends the weak, the stranger, and the oppressed, and teaches that this is as much an expression of God's essence as creating the Universe. Christ was poor, very poor, as in the "hood projects" poor, and spoke about money often—some say more than he did about salvation. Christ knew that your heart will be where your treasure is; therefore, if your heart is about influence, power, and money, then everything tends to be seen from that vantage point.

The American Church has lost its identity and has substituted a capitalistic agenda for Christ's agenda, all in the name of God. That is why God is not in a lot of our churches, because of this substitution. You hear tons of messages that center on provoking God to give to you as much as you give to him, and thus you will prosper and have individual material success. This avoids the central message of Jesus Christ to the poor. The American Church has sought to follow America as its God rather than the one true God, and its purpose is lost. You see the church grasping for gimmicks to keep folks coming to church, and using the capitalistic language and agenda of America. You even hear people saying, "We are church shopping." What happened to serving, dying to self, and doing life with others to build the kingdom of God?

According to the United Nations Human Development Report (2003), the richest 5 percent of the world's people receive 114 times as much income as the poorest 5 percent. In other words, twenty-five million Americans (the richest twenty-five million) enjoy as much income as the poorest two billion people in the world combined! Those who follow Christ should follow what he is passionate about, not what is popular or comfortable. Christians are to serve the poor, to love the least of these, to journey with each other in a community of faith, and live in wonder at how God meets our needs as we depend upon him and live interdependent with each other.

Scriptural reference(s):

Deuteronomy 8:1–16
Psalm 146
Matthew 6:19–24
Matthew 19:24
Matthew 25:31–46
Mark 10:24
Luke 4:16–21
Luke 18:25

Suggested additional sources:

- *Following Jesus through the Eye of the Needle* by Kent Annan
- *Counterfeit Gods* by Timothy Keller
- *Rich Christians in an Age of Hunger: Moving from Affluence to Generosity* by Ronald Sider

Questions for further discussion/thought:

1. How does Jesus' quote about rich people and the eye of the needle affect your goals in life?
2. Would you still desire to be rich even if it meant that others in the world must remain poor?
3. In what ways do you see Christians divesting themselves of power and privilege in order to be more like Christ?
4. Can those with wealth truly partner to serve alongside the least of these? How?
5. What does an authentic Acts 2 community look like today?

Sources cited:

- *The Holy Bible*
- *Rich Christians in an Age of Hunger: Moving from Affluence to Generosity* by Ronald Sider (Dallas: Word Publishing, 1997)
- *United Nations Human Development Report 2003*, available at http://hdr.undp.org/en/reports/global/hdr2003/

Where did all of the pictures of the blonde-haired, blue-eyed Jesus come from? Do Christians really think Jesus was white?

Adam J. Copeland

Who is...
Adam J. Copeland

I have eaten one peanut butter and jelly sandwich in my life. It was delicious.

A. Once when visiting the Iona Community in Scotland, I participated in a memorable workshop on just this question. Participants walked into a room filled with dozens of images of Jesus. Yes, there was that iconic Warner Sallman portrait with Jesus' long hair, beard, and blonde highlights, but there were also paintings of an Asian Jesus and Native American Jesus, African Jesus and an Irish-looking Jesus with red hair, feminine-looking Jesus and hyper-masculine Jesus, and, most accurately, a Middle Eastern Jesus. Taking in all those paintings was a moving experience for me. Among other things, it reminded me of how much culture affects our understanding of Scripture.

Later I learned about a group of forensic anthropologists who have attempted to create the "most accurate" image of Jesus. Using 3D imaging technology, scans of ancient skulls found near Jerusalem, and plenty of highly educated guesses, the team released a picture of what Jesus may have looked like. I was most struck, not by the skin tone, but the hair length: the scientists depict Jesus with short curly locks about the same length as his beard. They also suggest he may have stood 5 feet 1 inch (the average for the time) and weighed around 110 pounds.

It seems to be natural for cultures, as they relate to Jesus, to depict him as looking as they look. This probably says as much about our own sense of self as it does about our idea of Jesus. If Jesus is our most important friend and brother, and all our family and friends look like us, then it is not surprising that artists paint Jesus in their own image.

Phil Jackson

Yes, Christians really believe that Jesus is white, but he was not! So much of the art from the last 2000 years has Jesus with a pretty, white, blonde-haired, blue-eyed boyish face looking almost ghostly. Yet according to Isaiah 53:2 in *The Message Bible*, he was not attractive and nothing that would make us take a second look.

We have been kidnapped artistically by European artists who, to maintain control of their culture even in religious matters, painted pictures of a white Jesus. We have only been taught European Christianity from theologians, to preachers, to artists, and never truly get a world view of Christ, so when anyone paints another picture of Jesus other than the one we have seen forever, there is an automatic discomfort (for some) and almost hatred for the change of ethnicity (for others).

Ethiopian Christianity, which predates European Christianity, always has understood Jesus as African and that he has some African links. He grew up as a child in Egypt. If his skin was as pale as we have seen, then he would have stuck out and drawn more attention to himself. Skin that pale would have not been able to handle the sun nearly as well skin genetically provided with more melatonin in it, so as not to get burnt so often.

The fact is that Jesus was not white. He was a man whose color probably was more like Mediterranean men who have a darker hue. Dr. Goodacre, who was involved in the reconstruction of a Middle Eastern first-century skull for the BBC's *Son of God* program in 2001, said that the earliest images and pictures of Jews from the third century were all pretty much dark skinned. He also said, quoting Paul, that it was a disgrace for a man to have long hair, and that Christ didn't have long hair.

Christians have always been in need of an image of Christ, and sadly Europeans have tainted the truth that Christ was a man of color. This has brought some damage to those seeking reconciliation to God through Christ. I believe that the image of Christ being seen as a man of color is scary for most whites because it brings condemnation of their own racism. To stay safe, they paint him white.

Margot Starbuck

Though any self-respecting Christian would never *admit* we think Jesus is white, in the secret places of our hearts Christians like me totally do.

Though believers in my circles are much too sophisticated to suggest that someone who is native to the Middle East could have looked like he just hopped off a flight from Denmark, our imaginations have been saturated by images suggesting that very thing. Every picture I ever saw of Jesus as I was growing up—on church walls, or printed Sunday school lessons, or in children's picture Bibles—showed Jesus with long, straight, smooth-flowing European hair. Usually it was blonde. If a painted portrait allowed Jesus brown hair, it still had golden highlights. As for the eye situation, maybe Jesus' paternal genes just sort of overrode Mary's Middle Eastern ones since his heavenly Father obviously had blue eyes. Duh.

Though we'll never be caught dead admitting it, there is a foolproof test that reveals, to our own hearts anyway, our primal leanings when it comes to Jesus' ethnicity: hook yourself up to a heart monitor and then Google-image "black Jesus."

I thought so.

Jonathan Brooks

Once again, this blonde-haired, blue-eyed Jesus is another product of the wickedness of humanity. It stems again from the mistreatment of individuals and was birthed from the systemic lie that certain people are worth more than others. There is no way you could read the Bible, study history, research geography, or visit modern-day Palestine and believe Jesus was white, blonde-haired, or blue-eyed. But just like most history books of our time, this was a creation of a white male. We don't like to think of Jesus as he is described by scripture or history, but rather how we would like him to be. This has led minorities to oppose the typical portrait of Jesus, and we now see Jesus as a black man with dreadlocks, or an avid health nut on the cross with a six pack! The truth is the Bible gives us very little help in knowing Jesus' skin color, although we can infer he was a man of color due to the region in which he was born. The only passage that gives us a glimpse of the physical appearance of Christ is in Revelation, and it talks about Christ more in metaphoric terms. The earliest surviving Christian art comes from the late third and early fourth centuries on the walls of Christian tombs in the catacombs. Here they found some portraits of Jesus, usually with a long beard and long hair, which was the typical look of a Jewish man of his time

Scriptural reference(s):

Isaiah 53
1 Corinthians 11:14
Revelation 1:14–15

Suggested additional sources:

- *The Real Face of Jesus* by Mike Fillon, December 7, 2002 (especially the gallery) http://www.popularmechanics.com/science/health/forensics/1282186
- www.thenazareneway.com/likeness_of_our_savior.htm
- Google image searches: "Jesus" and "black Jesus"
- *So What Color Was Jesus?* http://news.bbc.co.uk/2/hi/3958241.stm
- *What Color Is Jesus?* by William Mosley

Questions for further discussion/thought:

1. How do you imagine Jesus when you consider him?
2. Does it bother you that other people picture a different image?
3. What sorts of feelings and thoughts are evoked in you when you encounter images of black Jesus? What about the Middle Eastern man seated next to you on a 747? Prayerfully notice this and invite God to teach you and transform your holy imagination.
4. Has the white captivity of the church tainted the truth of Jesus, theology, and history of the faith?

Sources cited:

- *The Real Face of Jesus* by Mike Fillon, December 7, 2002 (especially the gallery) http://www.popularmechanics.com/science/health/forensics/1282186
- *The Holy Bible*
- *So What Color Was Jesus?* http://news.bbc.co.uk/2/hi/3958241.stm

Two Friars and a Fool

It's hard for us to read the phrase "believe in science" without getting a little bit hot under the collar. Science is not a religion—it is the collective human effort to understand the world around us. The Latin *scientia* just means "knowledge"—science is a *way of knowing*. Science's agenda is very simple—to know more and understand more deeply.

Our history is brimming with famous scientists who were also people who held various faiths, including Christianity. Past Christians in science include Hildegard of Bingen, Pope Sylvester II, Roger Bacon, and Maria Gaetana Agnesi. Here and now, the current director of the Human Genome Project at the National Institutes of Health, mapping every gene in human DNA, is an Evangelical Christian named Dr. Francis Collins. Charles Hard Townes, a member of the United Church of Christ, writes about the relationship between science and religion, and won the Nobel Prize in Physics for his work in quantum electronics. Jennifer Wiseman is a Christian and chief of the ExoPlanets and Stellar Astrophysics Laboratory at NASA Goddard Space Flight Center.

There is no necessary conflict between the work of science and the life of faith. Most of the supposed conflict has come from the other direction—from people of faith responding to science with fear and aggression. Any human being, Christians included, who is interested in truth, in honest inquiry, and in growing in knowledge and understanding should not only "believe in science," but be excited by it.

Carol Howard Merritt

Who is...
Carol Howard Merritt

*As a teenager, I used to mime
as a form of evangelism.*

The poetry of Psalm 93 states that the world is firmly established, and it cannot be moved.

"And yet it moves," Galileo muttered under his breath as he was found "vehemently suspect of heresy" for having opinions that the earth revolves around the motionless sun.

Galileo's trial remains as a horrific stain on our church history, yet we keep playing out some version of this inquisition, over and over again. Religious leaders rail against high schools teaching evolution because it goes against the six-day creation account found in the Bible. Male church leaders cannot comprehend birth control, because they believe women stop the hand of God with that tiny pink pill. Even though many famous scientists are Christians, we often end up in that infuriating gridlock: religion versus science.

In premodern cultures, they understood that knowledge was obtained in different ways. Greeks described this as *logos* and *mythos*. *Logos* had a scientific quality, while *mythos* described something deeper. *Mythos* delved into the mysteries of human longing and understanding that cannot be covered in a scientific textbook.

The church struggled for centuries in the beauty and truth of *mythos*. Then, during the modern era, we mixed the two. We looked for scientific proof of God and tried to read our Scriptures as a chronological, historic, scientific account. Mangling the biblical narratives, we forced them into a false genre, while cheapening the truth of *mythos*.

The gift of the present time is that more people of faith are reclaiming the Bible as a holy text that speaks of a deeper truth.

Doug Pagitt

Who is...
Doug Pagitt

I have size 16 shoes.

Yes, a person can most certainly be a scientist and a Christian. There are many. For some there is a conflict between religion and science because they use different tools for discovering and understanding the world.

Science is a large category that covers many disciplines that use the "Scientific Method." The Scientific Method as described by Wikipedia is "a body of techniques for investigating phenomena, acquiring new knowledge, or correcting and integrating previous knowledge. To be termed scientific, a method of inquiry must be based on gathering empirical and measurable evidence subject to specific principles of reasoning."

Some more religiously minded people don't want to be limited to what can be discovered by this method. They are motivated by the understanding that there is more to the world than we can see or measure. "We walk by faith and not by sight" is often the claim.

The conflict comes when people from the two perspectives see their approach highly and the other rather lowly. There is a false battle between the two perspectives.

I believe that Science and Faith ought not to be married, but they need not be enemies either. They can be "friends with benefits." They have something crucial to offer one another.

Humanity uses scientific methodology to answer some of our questions, but not the totality of our questions. The same is true with faith.

Almost all Christians believe in science to some degree or they wouldn't believe in germs, own a computer, or use a GPS.

In the last century it has been the origin theories that create a point of struggle for some religious people. They don't know what to believe if the claims of science and faith on the origins of the cosmos and humanity are in conflict. This raises a concern that science answers the question, "Is there a God?" with a bold *no*.

In my view this need not be the case.

Scriptural reference(s):

Psalm 93

Suggested additional sources:

- *The Case for God* by Karen Armstrong
- "Karen Armstrong Builds a Case for God," in Fresh Air by Terry Gross and Karen Armstrong, September 21, 2009. http://www.npr.org/2009/09/21/112968197/karen-armstrong-builds-a-case-for-god
- *The Language of God* by Francis Collins
- http://en.wikipedia.org/wiki/List_of_Christian_thinkers_in_science
- http://www.templetonprize.org/pdfs/THINK.pdf
- *Quantum Theology* by Diarmuid O'Murchu

Questions for further discussion/thought:

1. When you look at passages such as Psalm 93, what genre would you say that it is in?
2. Discuss different literary devices, such as anthropomorphism, metaphor, and symbolism. Why do you think that authors use them?
3. What sort of genres and literary devices do we find in the Bible?
4. Aside from the Bible, what was the truest book, poetry, or play that you have ever read? Was it fiction or nonfiction?
5. Though the quote from Galileo is often cited, it may not be true. Why do you think it's such a famous quote?
6. In the Great Commandment, Jesus states: "Love the Lord your God with all your heart and with all your soul and with all your *mind*" (Mt. 22:37, NIV, emphasis added). Does fear of science, or the idea that science and faith are at odds, get in the way of loving God with our whole minds?
7. Can you think of a scientific discovery that might someday occur that would affect your faith—either making it stronger or undermining it?
8. Are there things that human beings were not meant to know? Questions human beings were not meant to ask? What are they, and why?

Source cited:

- *Thus Spoke Galileo: The Great Scientist's Ideas and Their Relevance to the Present Day* by Galileo Galilei, Andrea Frova, Mariapiera Marenzana (Oxford: Oxford University Press, 1998)

In too many instances, the most gracious, gentle, peaceful, thoughtful, patient, kind, generous, and steadfast people in my life have been non-Christians. Does it really take being a Christian to be Christlike?

Adam J. Copeland

A. My aunt and uncle are two of the kindest people I know. When it came time for their child to be baptized, my uncle decided he could not in good conscience participate fully in the service. He's an atheist—a gentle, thoughtful, generous, and loving atheist. At the baptism my uncle stood beside my aunt to support her, but he chose not to say "I do" at the usual moment. Neither did he pray. Even so, out of love for my aunt, my uncle supported her as my cousin was baptized into a faith he does not practice.

In many ways my uncle's life holds up the very essence of Christianity, but he is not a practicing Christian—or a Christian at all. My uncle might say he is a practicing humanist or one who intentionally practices love and justice, but to claim any other faith would be an affront to believers and nonbelievers alike.

Jesus once explained that the greatest commandment is to love God with all that we are, and the second is like it: to love our neighbors as ourselves. My uncle and many other non-Christians do their best to love their neighbors. This love, however, does not come in response to their love for God in Christ Jesus.

My uncle is a humble man. He would not like us to dwell on the fact that he lives out that second greatest commandment. Rather than pointing fingers at him for falling short on the first commandment, I simply try to keep up with him on the second.

Brian Ammons

A. Matthew 25 makes it pretty clear that Jesus had an understanding that some folks behaved in the ways that he would hope for all of us without ever framing it as serving him. When those gathered asked, "When did we feed you? When did we visit you in prison?" He responds, "Whenever you did it to the least of these, you did it to me." Considering that being Christlike—behaving like Jesus—might be more the point than affirming a particular confession of faith was a game-changer for me in my own spiritual life.

While I believe there is merit in intentionally claiming and being mentored in the living in the ways of Jesus, I also fully affirm that there are folks who come a lot closer to embodying Jesus' vision for a more just and loving world than I do—some of whom are neutral or even skeptical of the language of Christianity. As a Christian, I figure it's my work to look for the face of Jesus in each person I meet. I believe fully that it's there to be found.

Christian Piatt

Who is...
Christian Piatt

I once had a job cleaning out condemned apartment buildings.

This question begs a discussion about what it means to be a Christian. It seems like, for a long time, we accepted that only those who were regular members of a church were Christians. But then again, there are some people in particular denominations or churches who are quick to label others, whether they go to church or not, as not Christian, based on their own criteria.

While some people try to nail down the parameters by which we determine someone's identity as a Christian, I don't think it's ever that clear. For me, that's something each person has to decide for him- or herself; it's between that person and God. And from what I read in the gospel, that's what Jesus emphasized too.

Christianity is an orientation of the heart. It's an ever-changing yet particularly focused direction in which your life is pointed. Personally, I don't think God could care less whether you claim membership at a particular church or not. All of the trappings of religion are intended—at their best, at least—to help one orient one's life toward God by studying and imitating the life and teachings of Christ.

There are plenty of un-Christlike churchgoers, and there are plenty of people who follow the way of Jesus without claiming any certain Christian doctrine. The life you live says more about your faith than any denominational logo on a church door.

Sean Gladding

Who is...
Sean Gladding

I've ridden the same motorcycle for 20 years.

A. If being Christlike means to be gracious, gentle, peaceful etc., then the answer to the question is clearly "no." While I think Jesus was all those things, I don't think that such a list defines what it means to be "Christlike."

The Christ, the Son of God, was the one who would do what God's people, Israel, never could—which was to keep covenant with God, to do the will of God. Jesus said of himself, "the Son can do nothing of Himself, unless *it is* something He sees the Father doing; for whatever the Father does, these things the Son also does" (Jn. 5:19, NASB). Jesus calls those who do the will of God his family. What was the will of the Father for his life? "To preach the gospel to the poor[,] ...to proclaim release to the captives, and recovery of sight to the blind, to set free those who are oppressed, to proclaim the favorable year of the Lord" (Lk. 4:18–19, NASB). Apparently people who were not part of Jesus' followers were getting in on the act, much to his disciples' annoyance, but to Jesus' delight. There are also those apparently who do the will of God and don't even know it.

So the first question may really beg these two questions: "Why are some people who claim to be Christians such jerks?" and, "If to be Christlike is to do the will of God, then just who are the Christians?"

Scriptural reference(s):

Matthew 22:35–40
Matthew 25:31–46
Mark 3:34–35
Mark 12:28–34
Luke 4:18–19
Luke 9:49–50
Luke 10:25–28
John 5:19
The Gospels of Matthew, Mark, Luke, and John

Suggested additional sources:

- *A New Kind of Christian* by Brian McLaren
- *Following Jesus* by N. T. Wright
- *The Challenge of Jesus* by N. T. Wright
- *Who Will Be Saved?* By William H. Willimon

Questions for further discussion/thought:

1. What matters more: to *be* a Christian, or *act* like one?
2. Who in your life is Christlike, but not Christian?
3. Is being a Christian more about affirming particular beliefs or acting in particular ways? How do those two relate to one another?
4. Why are some people who claim to be Christians such jerks?
5. If to be Christ-like is to do the will of God, then just who are the Christians?

Source cited:

- *The Holy Bible*

Is Christianity really just about fire insurance? Are we just trying to make sure we don't go to hell when we die? And if personal salvation is a once-and-for-all event, why bother taking part in church after that?

Jonathan Brooks

When Jesus is asked what is the most important commandment, he responds with, "Love God with everything and love your neighbor as yourself" (Mt. 22:37–39, paraphrase). No guarantees, magic prayers, sacred ceremonies, or other rituals that get you a "get-out-of-hell-free card." Christianity is about a daily, loving relationship with God and the people around you.

When two people get married, they begin their marital relationship at a wedding, but then the marriage begins. You are not in a committed marital relationship with someone because you had a wedding. If so, you could have the ceremony and then never see each other again. God offers us the opportunity to connect with him through Jesus and trust him every day of our lives. This is not for the sole purpose of going to heaven or not going to hell. It is for the purpose of knowing and enjoying God every moment of our lives from that moment forward. Jesus reminds us that we are called to love the people around us in the same way.

Christianity is not about reserving an eternal five-star hotel room when we die. It is about recognizing the great opportunity to have a relationship with God through Jesus Christ. No matter who you are or where you live, you can have unlimited access to God! This great honor and opportunity are part of the reason we take part in church. It's an opportunity to hang out with people who are as excited about this opportunity as you are.

Phil Shepherd, *a.k.a.* The Whiskey Preacher

Who is...
Phil Shepherd

I am allergic to spinach;
it makes my lips blow up.

I think Jesus was a contextual teacher; in other words, he used imagery familiar to those he was teaching. Being a contextual teacher, he used props—tangible illustrations—a lot. Jesus, in my humble opinion, who I respect (it's okay to laugh here…I am), used imagery that was known to the crowds that he was teaching. Communicating the idea of hell was no different. Jesus used a commonly known local prop—the fiery dump outside of Jerusalem—to create the imagery of what's opposite of the kingdom of heaven: a fiery heap of shit where even worms won't die.

I don't think Jesus or the followers of Jesus intended for hell to become what we have created it into. Hell is this: the opposite of the kingdom of heaven. Hell is the opposite of loving the Creator and loving the creation. Hell is rejecting the notion that God not only made us "good" but "really good," a statement that God never recanted.

Christianity is not about fire insurance or avoiding going to hell, but about living into the kingdom of heaven. Hell and the kingdom of heaven are in the here-and-now, not some hereafter. The kingdom of heaven is loving the Creator, loving the creation, and embracing the fact we are made in the image of God, the God who calls us "good, really good."

We were not created to journey alone, but *with* one another, exfoliating the kingdom of heaven as we go, a journey many of us call Christianity.

Sean Gladding

It certainly seems that over the course of the last couple of centuries many streams of the church have reduced the epic Story scripture narrates to the question of individual salvation: "fire insurance." And the decline in the culture of church-going indicates that people neither find that version of the story, nor "church as we know it," compelling.

My conviction is that the gospel most of us have encountered, both in its proclamation and in the life of the church that does the proclaiming, is a pale shadow of the Story told in scripture. That Story is one in which the Creator God refuses to abandon God's good creation to the consequences and effects of human sin, but rather intends to save the world through a people, the

25

family of Abraham, the nation of Israel. But Israel was part of the problem, so God assumed the problem as God's own, becoming one of us in the person of Jesus of Nazareth. Jesus lived the life that Israel could not, and then took all the brokenness of humanity upon himself, dying that all might be forgiven and that all things might be made new. With his resurrection began new creation, and in the sending of the Holy Spirit came the power to live a life in which we partner with God in the ongoing work of new creation. The Story ends not in avoiding hell and ascending into heaven, but in God descending once more to live with us in the new creation forever.

Scriptural reference(s):

Genesis 1:31
Genesis 12:1–3
Exodus 19:3–6
Matthew 22:37–40
The Gospels of Matthew, Mark, Luke, and John
Philippians 2:1–13
1 Peter 2:9–10
Revelation 21:1–5; 22:1–5

Suggested additional sources:

- *Are You My Neighbor?* by Dr. Wayne Gordon
- *Salvation Means Creation Healed* by Howard Snyder
- *The King Jesus Gospel* by Scot McKnight
- *Surprised by Hope* by N. T. Wright
- *The Story We Find Ourselves In* by Brian McLaren
- *The Story of God, the Story of Us* by Sean Gladding
- *Discovering the God Imagination* by Jonathan Brink

Questions for further discussion/thought:

1. If this sums up Christianity, how should this change the way we live and look at those who are not very loving but claim to be Christians?
2. What "Story" do you think the Bible is telling?
3. Why do some people still find the "fire insurance" version of the story so attractive?
4. How do you think you are invited to partner with God in the work of new creation in your context? And with whom could you do that?
5. What and where is hell for you?

6. Do you believe that we are still a good creation even after what happened in the garden with Adam and Eve?
7. How do you experience the kingdom of heaven in the here and now?

Source cited:

- *The Holy Bible*

Some Christians believe the Bible is without error and the only real authority for living, but they ignore parts of the Old and New Testament. Why hold on to six verses on homosexuality but ignore books and chapters about slavery?

Andrew Marin

A. Too many Christians practice an incorrect style of interpretation: verse-focused theology over principled theology. A verse-focused theology centers around a single verse, or a group of individual verses, that repeat approximately the same sentence. It is singular and capsulated in a time and place. This interpretation style makes certain messages easier to remember, and thus lends to Christians picking-and-choosing what they choose to remember as most important.

A principled theology focuses on eternal principles throughout Scripture that are applicable in any time and any place, to any people. These principles are easier to notice in the New Testament because we are still living under the new covenant, but what about the Old Testament's strange rules and regulations? The best way to hone in on an eternal principle is through the following: the principle must (1) be reflected in the biblical text; (2) not be tied to a specific situation; (3) not be culturally bound to a specific date, time, situation, or group of people; (4) correspond to the teaching of the rest of Scripture; and (5) be relevant to both biblical and contemporary audiences.

Through such an understanding, all of the Old Testament applies to new covenant Christians by way of eternal principles. The difficulty is that principled theology is more nuanced and takes much more time spent studying and meditating on the intricacies of Scripture. Through a principled theology one can still holistically hold the Bible, Old and New, as the real authority for living.

Bart Campolo

Who is...
Bart Campolo

I hate filling out questionnaires.

Here is my open admission of what seems to me a universal characteristic of those of us who call ourselves Christians:

Coming to the Bible with an a priori understanding of who God is and how God works that is the product of my cultural and personal influences, my spiritual and moral intuitions, my experiences and observations of the world around me, and my deepest emotional and psychological needs, I underline, interpret, and even ignore various passages in accordance with that understanding, believing that God is guiding me in that process as a form of divine communication.

We Christians have always done that, of course, whether or not we admitted it. Those who once owned slaves confidently underlined one set of Bible passages, while those who worked to abolish slavery just as eagerly underlined another, very different set of passages, and each side interpreted away or ignored the verses that contradicted their *a priori* paradigm of God. For better and worse, these divine paradigms, whether consciously or unconsciously adopted, are what really determine the way we read the Bible on complicated issues such as capital punishment, war, the role of women, economic justice, divorce, gay marriage, and the essential character of Jesus.

The main difference between me and those who call me a heretic is that I am both conscious and unashamed of the fact that my elemental faith in a good and loving God is not based on biblical authority. In fact, just the opposite is true. I trust the Bible only because of and only to the degree to which it corresponds with my foundational, extra-biblical, *a priori* faith. In other words, I listen to and preach from the Bible not because I think it is clear, coherent, consistent, inerrant, or divinely dictated, but rather because both history and my own experience have convinced me that God fairly consistently chooses to speak through it, in spite of the fact that it is none of those things.

29

Brian Ammons

We all read through cultural lenses. There is no avoiding it. Regardless of whether or not we own it, our context shapes the way we engage scripture. I tend to approach the Bible as a library rather than as a single book. There are lots of authors, each trying to convey particular truths about how God was being revealed to them. Each one, in turn, became part of how God is revealed to us, but the Bible is not a static text. It is so powerful precisely because it has this unique history of being read and reread, translated and interpreted, as communities have looked to it to help understand their experience of sacred mystery. That is the work of the living body of Christ resurrected in the life of the church…and it's pretty amazing.

Phil Shepherd, *a.k.a.* The Whiskey Preacher

I am a man of convenience, and I am not ashamed to admit it. At Christmastime, I love using my Amazon Prime account as my surrogate "Santa-zon"* to deliver presents directly to the doors of friends and family, all wrapped and ready to be placed under the tree. And let's not forget about the convenience of adult butt-wipes, heaven-sent, that keep me going through the swamp-butt months (better known as Texas summer). Conveniences are all around us, and we have learned to justify their existence because they make our lives easier. Let's face it: I don't actually "need" Amazon Prime to play "Santa-zon," but it makes the holidays easier for me.

I think that this is how we (I am including myself in this) sometimes approach Scripture: with convenience. It's easier than getting our hands dirty, digging around to find out what the whole story is trying to communicate. When we don't seek out the whole story, we create piecemeal observations, which in turn create piecemeal arguments and conclusions.

Did you know that it wasn't until the late 1940s that the word *homosexuality* was integrated into English translations of the Bible?** Because of convenience, many of us have no idea of this little-known fact, yet many of us have created entire theological structures and arguments out of our unwillingness to do a little work. We end up creating scapegoats—whether it's slavery, divorce, secular music, homosexuality, or *fill-in-the-blank*—because it's the convenient, easier option to choose.

---

*Santa-zon: A clever term coined by my sister-in-law, Dianna Shirley, during Christmas of 2011.

***Revised Standard Version** (RSV) 1946 is the first English translation of the Bible to use the word *homosexual* in its translation.

Scriptural reference(s):

Mark 13:31
John 1

Suggested additional sources:

- *Jesus, The Bible, and Homosexuality* by Jack Rogers (progressive)
- *Slaves, Women and Homosexuals* by William Webb (conservative)
- *The Blue Parakeet* by Scot McKnight
- *Free for All: Rediscovering the Bible in Community* by T. Conder and D. Rhodes
- *Queering Christ: Beyond Jesus Acted Up* by R. Goss
- *Reading from This Place: Social Location and Biblical Interpretation in the United States* by F. Segovia and M.A. Tolbert
- *The New Kind of Trilogy* by Brian McLaren
- *Gay Conversations With God* by James Langteaux

Questions for further discussion/thought:

1. What are some principles that consistently run throughout the Old and New Testaments, regardless of what the word-on-the-page story is specifically addressing?
2. Who is in your "interpretive community"? Who are the people you listen to or trust most about how they read Scripture? Who is not represented in your interpretive community?
3. Is there a healthier way to engage Scripture, and if so what does that look like for you and your community?
4. If we have we misinterpreted the verses on homosexuality in our English translations, how does that change the way Christians interact with the GLBTQ community?
5. In the first chapter of the Gospel of John, it proclaims that Jesus is the Word of God yet many call the Bible the word of God. Why is that?

Source cited:

- *Grasping God's Word* by J. Scott Duvall and J. Daniel Hayes (Grand Rapids, Mich.: Zondervan, 2001)

Are Mormons, Jehovah's Witnesses, Seventh Day Adventists, Spiritists, Christian Scientists, etc., really Christians? Who gets to decide?

Doug Pagitt

Who is...
Doug Pagitt

I'm an Enneagram 8.

A. The question of who gives approval for someone claiming to be a follower of Jesus has unfortunately been part of the faith from its founding. Jesus' disciples were accused of not being part of the faith of Abraham since they prayed wrongly. They, in turn, thought that those who were not doing faith their way were out, only to be corrected by Jesus that "whoever isn't against us is for us."

Christianity is not a faith in which there are certain cultural or belief quotas that must be met; rather, it is an opt-in faith. A people are part of the Christian tradition when they declare themselves to be.

Not only was it that way at the time of Jesus, it was so in the years afterward.

Christian is a cultural term assigned first to people in Antioch in the first century, and it is described in the book of the Bible called Acts in Chapter 11 verse 26. We are given a little nugget of understanding for how the term Christian was first used. It was given to non-Jewish followers of Jesus in Antioch who were following the teachings of Paul. But the Jewish believers did not consider these "Christians" to be a true part of the faith, so the term was used first to exclude them from the faith. Only later did it become the term used almost universally.

With the development over the last two thousand years of many versions of Christianity in varied cultures with opt-in faith beliefs, there is no standard-bearing group that gets to speak on behalf of all Christian traditions. Christianity is a faith in which all professions are included. In the words of Peter from the first century, we are all invited to see that "I really am learning that God doesn't show partiality to one group of people over another" (Acts 10:34, CEB).

Jonathan Brooks

This is a very touchy topic, because I personally would not place all of these groups into the same category. There are some basic things that you must hold to in order to be a Christian as defined by Jesus Christ himself. Some would say if they don't agree with repentance, acceptance of Christ's sacrifice, and unconditional love, Christ would tell us to wipe the dust off our feet and keep moving.

Personally, my issue with certain religious groups is really not their theology as much as their thoughts about people. Any religion that looks at one group as inferior to another, in my consideration, is not Christianity. Jehovah's Witnesses and Mormons have traditionally looked upon minorities as inferior to whites and are distinctly American religions. Prior to 1978, Mormons forbid blacks from joining the Mormon Church. I personally don't know who gets to decide whether they are Christians or not, but if you ask them, they will say emphatically that they are.

Seventh Day Adventists seem to follow the same guidelines as most Christians but add a Saturday Sabbath and dietary restrictions. I think additional preferences and denial of human rights are two very different issues, so I would not place them in the same category.

Each group must stand alone, and you as an individual must decide which groups are Christian according to your standards. I urge you to do your homework, and I think you will find we all have just as much in common as we have differences.

Scriptural reference(s):

Matthew 7:22
Matthew 24:4–5
Acts 10:34
Galatians 1:8
Galatians 3:28

Suggested additional sources:

- *So What's the Difference?* by Fritz Ridenour
- *Kingdom of the Cults* by Dr. Walter Martin
- *Know What You Believe* by Paul E. Little

Do Christians have to be baptized? Why do some sprinkle while others immerse? Which one is "right"?

Brian Ammons

Who is...
Brian Ammons

My folks worked at a Children's Home and I was raised on campus.

I'm a Baptist minister who was baptized (sprinkled) as an infant in the United Methodist Church. I've never been "re-baptized" through immersion, and though the tradition I claim as an adult follows an immersion practice, I value deeply my infant baptism. For me, to have been claimed as a child of God, beloved, sacred, and holy, before I had the language to even speak my name is a powerful and beautiful image. That blessing is mine, and no one can take it away from me. At times when I've felt some pretty vicious attacks coming from the church, that knowledge sustained me.

At the same time, I have stood chest deep in the baptismal waters with young adults resting back in my arms. I know the deep power and beauty of the "Believer's Baptism" ritual. Experiencing the profound abandon and deep trust that bodily submerging and emerging offers is tangible metaphor for a deeply profound inner experience. I feel immensely grateful to have been invited into that process with the people I lowered into and lifted out of those waters.

At this point in my journey, I am less tied to sacrament than I am to the sacramental. That is to say that I am less bound to the idea that there is a literal transformation in the baptismal process, the kind of thinking that gets really concerned about getting it right, but I am still invested in the idea that the ritual (whether sprinkled, poured, or immersed) is an outward and visible sign of an inward, transformational grace.

Margot Starbuck

Who is...
Margot Starbuck

I did a Slurpee "world tour" road trip with
two of my kids this summer (ill-advised).

Sprinkling is right. Whatever monkey business God does in baptism should definitely be moderated. Those hippy Jesus People in the seventies got dunked and went *way* overboard. In fact, even when sprinkling, have a towel nearby to wipe off any excess. Immediately.

Wait, did I say that out loud?

I meant: Dunking is right. Faith isn't just a top-of-the-*head* thing. It's something that you commit to with your whole being. If you're not dunked then you're probably holding back and not giving everything to Jesus. Dunking shows real commitment, because Jesus was dunked, not sprinkled.

I said that, too, didn't I?

The earliest Christian baptisms symbolized being plunged under dangerous waters into *death* with Christ. Dead—not *mostly* dead, but *dead*-dead—the believer is resurrected to new life with Christ. The old is gone and the believer's life is now a function of Christ's life within him or her. It's like the way Disney princesses, such as Snow White and Sleeping Beauty, slumber off into death and, once rescued, their lives then become a function of their rescuer-redeemer—for better or for worse.

Both sprinkling and dunking are physical signs of dying and rising to life with Christ. And though Christians too often make it about the christening gown or the catered after-party, it's really a fundamental sign of our Christian identity, meant to guide and form our Christlike living. Not to be a downer, but a life patterned after the cross of Christ is sort of…death-shaped—for better or for worse.

Scriptural reference(s):

Matthew 3:16

Suggested additional sources:

- *Grace for the Journey: Interpreting Baptist Ordinances for the 21st Century* by Cathy Tamsberg http://www.sitemason.com/files/fjcRTW/ Grace%20for%20the%20Journey.pdf
- *This Gift of Water: The Practice and Theology of Baptism among Methodists in America* by G. Felton
- http://en.wikipedia.org/wiki/Baptism

Questions for further discussion/thought:

1. What is the role of ritual in shaping our understanding of belonging to a community? What does it mean to belong?
2. Would you be able to give a persuasive argument for dunking? Sprinkling? Try to argue from the position you do not hold.

Question

It seems like there's a lot of conflict between Christians and Jews. Wasn't Jesus Jewish? Aren't Christians technically Jewish too?

Christian Piatt

A. It's interesting how hung up on such distinctions people get, such as Jew, Christian, Muslim, citizen, immigrant, and so on. I think it's especially important when talking about those who call themselves "Christians," and who claim the Bible, and particularly the New Testament, as foundational to their lives and identity.

It's easy to forget that Jesus wasn't a Christian. After all, he didn't follow himself! And the early followers of Christ, even after his death, didn't see themselves as no longer Jewish, though others might have seen them as acting in violation of Jewish law. But culturally, they were Jews.

Even Paul, the author credited for much of the writing found in the New Testament, asserts in Galatians 3:28 that such distinctions should, and do, fall away in the context of Jesus' life, death, and resurrection. What I think Paul is saying is that what you call yourself isn't the point. Jesus has broken down such barriers, as indicated when the temple curtain was torn apart upon Christ's death. The divisions between God and us were removed.

So why do we keep trying so hard to rebuild them, between us and God, but also between us and our brothers and sisters?

Carol Howard Merritt

A. Kevin's head thumped against the door of the bathroom stall, as he sweated over his fate. Engaged to an Orthodox Jewish woman, Kevin promised he would convert. After completing the required classes, he faced the last hurdle: circumcision. He looked down at himself and, like a foxhole atheist, Kevin whispered to God, "If you get me out of this, I swear I'll go to seminary."

Kevin enrolled in seminary, as a single man, the next fall.

I met Kevin in grad school. It was also within the walls of the theological institution that I learned how much our past is poisoned with anti-Semitism. Perusing Martin Luther's *Table Talks*, I found his work engorged with vile bigotry.

After the horrors of World War II, Christian leaders strengthened their interfaith relationships and critiqued the hatred that we perpetuated against

Jews. Yet, anti-Semitism continues as a dark part of our tradition, one that we continually need to expose, challenge, and expunge.

Jesus was Jewish, and Christianity began as a sect of Judaism. Many of our earliest controversies had to do with whether Gentiles would be allowed to be a part of Christianity. And much of it came down to the question, Would Gentile converts to Christianity have to be circumcised?

As Kevin understood, being circumcised as a grown man is a much bigger hurdle than walking down to the altar during the sixth round of "Just as I Am." And I'm not even going to imagine what that operation would have been like with ancient surgical tools and anesthesia. The great gift of Paul was that he welcomed Gentiles, struggling to make sure that circumcision was not a requirement for conversion. Now, Christians have an important job of making sure that we nurture our interfaith understandings and renounce our anti-Semitism.

Margot Starbuck

Great question. Why don't you ask an orthodox Jew?

No, no! Just kidding! Don't do it!

You've asked two very different questions here that need to be addressed separately.

Though anti-Semitic Christians have attempted to de-Jewify Jesus, he indeed was Jewish. Any of our leanings to either suggest that he wasn't or to conveniently forget it reveal more about us than they do about Jesus.

From day one, God's plan was that salvation would come to the world through a Jewish Messiah sent to God's chosen people, the Jews. This said, what happened *after* Jesus' life, death, resurrection, and ascension, namely the forming of a new body, had to have felt a little whiplash-y to believing Jews and Gentiles alike. As the church was being formed, everyone was trying to figure out if Gentiles needed to become Jewish, a.k.a. be circumcised, in order to be Christians. (The very question would have made a lot of Gentile dudes into deeply prayerful men.) Though there was some disagreement, the final answer of the early church was a decisive NO. Gentiles did *not* need to perform religious rites to become Jewish before becoming Christians.

Though Messianic Jewish Christians are fully Jewish and fully Christian, the rest of us are not. We do, however, claim the fullness of God's story that is woven throughout Jewish history. In this sense, the Jews are most certainly "our people."

Scriptural reference(s):

Romans 2:25–29
1 Corinthians 7:18
Galatians 3:28
Galatians 5:2
The Epistle to the Galatians
Ephesians 2

Suggested additional sources:

- *The Jewish Annotated New Testament* by Amy-Jill Levine and Mark Brettler
- http://en.wikipedia.org/wiki/Council_of_Jerusalem

Questions for further discussion/thought:

1. What do you think it means to be a Christian?
2. Which is more important: living a Christlike life, or identifying as a Christian? Or can you even have one without the other?
3. Do you have people with different religious beliefs in your family? What have you learned from them? Are there practices from other religious traditions that you appreciate?
4. Can you name a time in history when religious intolerance has incited political unrest?
5. How can understanding between religions bring increased diplomacy in our world events?
6. How do you react when you see anti-Semitism in Christian thought?
7. Besides circumcision, what sorts of issues would the earliest Jewish Christians and Gentile Christians have faced together, as one new body?

Source cited:

- "Of the Jews," *Table Talks*, Martin Luther, http://www.reformed.org/master/index.html?mainframe=/documents/Table_talk/table_talk.html

If all Christians basically believe the same thing, why do they have so many different denominations? And if there are so many denominations struggling to survive, why don't they just combine with other ones?

Hugh Hollowell

Who is...
Hugh Hollowell

Despite having been a Marine, I am a Mennonite pastor, devoted to nonviolence.

It is frustrating, isn't it? In a perfect world, we would all be one. In fact, Jesus prayed for that very thing. The reality is there are many different ways to engage a life of faith, and most denominations tend to focus on one over the others. and most people end up in the denomination that makes sense of how they engage God.

For example, Episcopalians tend to focus on liturgy or the ceremonies of the church, while Mennonites tend to focus on what happens during the week and in their community, and Presbyterians tend to be interested in scholarship. All three are legitimate ways of engaging God.

There are folks like myself who come to know things primarily through our bodies, so being Mennonite makes sense to me. Others are wired in such a way that they know things primarily by engaging their five senses, so the chanting and bells of the Episcopalians make more sense to them. Still others tend to live in their heads, so they want to know what the word was in the original Greek. These people are probably happy as Presbyterians. None of these are wrong—just different.

Most people are not that predictable in their church searching. It is just that we tend to end up at places that feel comfortable to us, and those places tend to have other people like us there.

Margot Starbuck

Throughout the centuries, various groups of Christians have, in essence, said, "In order to be in the club, you need to believe X, Y, Z." Sometimes, X, Y, and Z were issues core to the Christian faith. They were things such as, "Jesus' mom was a virgin," "Jesus is God's son," "Jesus rose from the dead," and "You don't get into heaven simply by paying money to the Church." They were clearly deal-breakers.

What's a deal-breaker for some folks, such as dunk baptisms or sprinkle baptisms, isn't a deal-breaker for others. Centuries of Church divisions have happened because some group of Christians truly believed in their hearts that whatever reason they were leaving over—a literal seven-day creation, women serving in church leadership, ordination of LGBTQ folks—really was, for them, a deal-breaker. So, while Christ's heart for his Church is unity, many Christians have had to follow their consciences and…split.

I think your suggestion for denominations to combine is just genius. While I suspect the answer for some in these smaller bodies who retain a clear memory of exactly what caused a local split and how very wrong the other side was is, "When hell freezes over," it's not unheard of. In the town where I live, I can point to two instances in the last five years of churches that split years ago being reunited under one holy roof. That, I am convinced, is a sign of the Kingdom.

Scriptural reference(s):

John 17:18
1 Corinthians 1:10

Questions for further discussion/thought:

1. If you had to trim down the "deal-breakers" to a bare minimum, what would they be?
2. What are the nonnegotiable essentials that you believe are central to the Christian faith?

Can someone be both an atheist and a Christian? If "Christian" actually means "follower of Christ," could someone be a student of the life of Jesus without accepting the claims of his divinity, or claims of the existence of any divinity at all?

Jonathan Brooks

Who is...
Jonathan Brooks

I love the smell of gasoline.

A. I suppose someone could follow Jesus in his humanity alone, although it is a bit of an oxymoron. It is very possible for people to be followers of Christ's moral teachings and still be atheists because they do not believe that Christ claimed to be God, and interpret those scriptures differently.

Jesus offers us so much more than mere wisdom. He offers us access to something and someone far greater. Jesus tells us in John that we must stay connected to him in order to produce the outcomes of his teachings, so trusting him as Lord is part of trusting him as teacher. My friend Brad would say it this way: *You are a toaster and God is the socket. Unless you stay plugged in to him, you will not toast anything.* Although having a toaster in our kitchen, admiring it, and reading the manual about all of the great toast it makes would be fine, it would still be weird to never plug it in to its power source and see it really do its job—toast things. To me, this is equivalent to following Jesus in his humanity and not believing in his deity. You can get great teachings and gain great knowledge, but the power behind those words comes from the Spirit of God. The Spirit of God is gained through accepting Jesus as Lord and Savior.

Phil Snider

Who is...
Phil Snider

I really don't like to blog, and I'm envious of folks like Christian who are so good at it.

There are a lot of people who value Jesus' teachings but have a hard time accepting claims of his divinity. Depending on how you interpret Jesus' words in Mark 10:18 ("Why do you call me good?… No one is good—except God alone" [NIV]), even Jesus himself was hesitant to accept claims of his own divinity.

By the time the Gospel of John was written (several years after Mark was written), storytellers had become much more concerned with portraying Jesus as divine. When we hear verses such as John 14:6 ("I am the way and the truth and the life. No one comes to the Father except through me" [NIV]), it leads us to think that only those who believe in God ("the Father") can be a Christian. Yet according to Frederick Buechner, if we pay close attention, Jesus "didn't say that any particular ethic, doctrine, or religion was the way, the truth, and the life. He said that he was. He didn't say that it was by believing or doing anything in particular that you could 'come to the Father.' He said that it was only by him—by living, participating in, being caught up by, the way of life that he embodied, that was his way." All of which leads Buechner to conclude that it's "possible to be on Christ's way and with his mark upon you without ever having heard of Christ, and for that reason to be on your way to God though maybe you don't even believe in God."

Two Friars and a Fool

Many people already self-identify as both atheist and Christian. Groups such as the Christian Humanists and Non-Theistic Christians are doing just that—following Jesus, practicing Christianity, but for the most part holding to a naturalistic worldview where there is no supernatural or transcendent God.

In fact, the earliest Christians were called atheists by their neighbors because they refused to worship anyone but Christ. There is an anti-superstition impulse deep in the heart of Christianity. As Peter Rollins likes to say, to believe is human; to doubt is divine.

It is true, though, that the Jesus we read about in the Gospels seems to have believed in a transcendent, supernatural God, and is described as

43

performing acts we would now call miracles—such as restoring sight to the blind, walking on water, and so on. For some Christians, it is necessary for these things to be historically true. God must be in some way outside the world, and also able to act directly in the world.

For other Christians this is not as important. We don't call ourselves Non-Theistic Christians or Christian Humanists, but we don't have a problem calling people who do identify that way brothers and sisters in Christ. They can be more than just students of the life of Jesus—they can be "doers of the Word." They can live out the title "Christian," "little Christs," in their daily lives just as well as we can.

Scriptural reference(s):

Matthew 21:28–32
Mark 10:18
John 14:6

Suggested additional sources:

- www.atheists-for-jesus.com
- *The Human Being* by Walter Wink
- *Wishful Thinking* by Frederick Buechner
- www.christianhumanist.net
- http://www.nontheistfriends.org/

Questions for further discussion/thought:

1. Does it take credibility away from Christ's other teachings if you deny his claims of his own divinity?
2. Is Christianity primarily about belief or action? Why or why not? Is it possibly a combination of both? If so, why?
3. In the parable of the two sons, Jesus says that God is happier with the son who is wrong in word but right in deed than with the son who is right in word but wrong in deed. What do you think this may have to say about Christians and atheists?
4. Whether you think an atheist can be a Christian or not, what do you see as the minimum a person must believe, say, or do in order to be a Christian?

Sources cited:

- *The Holy Bible*
- *Wishful Thinking* by Frederick Buechner (New York: Harper & Row, 1973), p. 14
- *Insurrection* by Peter Rollins (Nashville: Howard Books, 2011)

Why do so many churches do communion in different ways and on such different schedules? Who is allowed to serve communion? And do all Christians believe the bread and wine/juice actually become the body and blood of Jesus? Why?

Brian Ammons

Who is...
Brian Ammons

I'm slightly obsessed with Dolly Parton.

These are complicated questions that have long, complex (and sometimes violent) histories behind them. The differences in our communion practices tend to be grounded in the differences in how we understand what is actually happening in the ritual of communion.

In my congregation, we operate from the understanding that the table is God's table, and, as God's grace is freely extended to all, all are welcome at the table. Because we affirm the priesthood of all believers, different members of the community preside at the table, and frequently the children are involved in serving. When I take the bread and cup, I understand it as a way of ritually embodying my participation in the resurrected body of Christ, alive and well in the life of the church. It is the central ritual in our community, and we practice it each time we gather.

So that's one end of the spectrum. I feel a bit uneasy about speaking for another tradition, but I can say that I respect that communion practices that require only ordained clergy to preside, or only baptized people to partake, make sense if one holds a different understanding of what the bread and wine actually are doing. The less metaphorical the understanding, the greater the need to safeguard the elements.

Doug Pagitt

Communion, the Lord's supper, the Eucharist has been part of the Christian tradition from the start. But it has also been practiced by Christians in different ways, with different meanings from the start. There is no universally right way to do it, or right meaning of it. Some use wine and others use juice. Some use bread with yeast and other do not. Some practice it daily, others annually.

Communion had its origin in the Jewish Passover celebration that Jesus practiced. Then it became part of the "Love Feast" culture in the first century. Then it became a practice of the Church in the third century.

There simply is no one meaning for nor one way to practice communion, Eucharist, the Lord's supper, or whatever you may call it.

Scriptural reference(s):

Matthew 27.17-29
Mark 14.12-25
Luke 22.7-23
1 Corinthians 11.23-36

Suggested additional sources:

- *The Sacred Meal* by N. Gallagher
- *Grace for the Journey: Interpreting Baptist Ordinances for the 21st Century* by Cathy Tamsberg, http://www.sitemason.com/files/fjcRTW/Grace%20for%20the%20Journey.pdf

Questions for further discussion/thought:

1. What are some of the experiences that you've had around the supper table?
2. What is the power in sharing a meal with other people?

What do Christians believe about disaster and suffering in the world? If God has a plan, why is suffering part of it? How do Christians reconcile suffering in their own lives?

Andrew Marin

A. Unexpected deaths. Shattered dreams. Infertility. Betrayals. Unmet goals and prayers. Like anyone else I have had my share of suffering that can't be explained by any rational thought process. So how do I still have a faith in a God that I believe has a good plan? Because God never said, let alone promised, there would be no suffering. In fact, the Bible says just the opposite.

I believe people use suffering as an easy excuse to blame God, to point the finger at someone else, or to not have faith at all. Those are all too easy options of escapism. For me, suffering is an opportunity to actually live my faith when it matters the most. Anyone can live a good faith when things are great. Suffering doesn't make life or faith easy, right, justified, or satisfying. It makes it real.

In the midst of my pain and often-cried tears I can still call God's name and be thankful for an opportunity to live and feel and try to love through it all. In the midst of suffering is when I've been most real with God. I have nowhere else to turn; no one else to call upon. It's me and God. Together. Not in some cliché way that God will make it all better, but a hopeless-filled place where the rubber meets the road by practicing what I preach. In some twisted way it's where I feel connected to God the most.

Matthew Paul Turner

Who is...
Matthew Paul Turner

I can do a split.

The disciples asked Jesus a multiple choice question: Why was this man born blind? Was it (a) because he had sinned, or (b) because his parents had sinned? Jesus refuses both of their karmic options and proposes that the man's blindness presents an opportunity for God's glory to be shown. No, Mark Driscoll, I don't think he's indicating that God caused the man to go through a lifetime of blindness because one day Jesus was going to happen to walk by, and he would need someone to perform a miracle on to impress his friends. I think Jesus is reframing the entire scenario. What if Jesus is suggesting that suffering isn't an intellectual dilemma in need of a satisfying explanation? As anyone who has truly suffered knows, explanations of suffering aren't really that helpful. What if, instead, Jesus is suggesting that any instance of suffering presents an opportunity for those who would follow this God to partner with him in bringing healing into sickness, light into darkness, hope into despair.

The Bible doesn't attempt to offer a satisfying answer to the question of suffering. Instead, it describes a God who suffers with us and issues a call for us to embody a response rather than offer an explanation. We are not to insulate ourselves from suffering. We are to be the ones who enter into the suffering of others to help them bear it. As agents of hope, it is our calling to reflect and embody this God where he cannot be easily found.

Hugh Hollowell

Who is...
Hugh Hollowell

I only wear grey and blue.
On fancy days, I include black.

In my own faith, I have found it most helpful to think of it like this: God does have a plan to deal with the hungry children in Africa, a plan to ease the suffering of the sick, a plan to feed the hungry, a plan to comfort the afflicted.

God has a plan, and God's plan is us.

That children are hungry in a world where one in three of us are obese is not a failure of God, but a failure of us to live up to our part of God's plan. Often, Christians pray for God to act to ease suffering, when it is, in fact, God who waits on us to act.

Scriptural reference(s):

John 15:20
Romans 5:3–5
1 Peter 4:12

Suggested additional sources:

- *A Theology of the Dark Side* by Nigel Goring Wright
- *Come Be My Light* by Mother Teresa
- *Evil and the Justice of God* by N. T. Wright
- *Friendship at the Margins* by Christopher Heuertz and Christine Pohl

Questions for further discussion/thought:

1. What is the first thing you do when you feel suffering?
2. Talk about the unanswered questions you still have about times of suffering in your life.

Source cited:

- *The Holy Bible*

I've met lots of people who say they are Christian but haven't been to church in a long time. I've even met some who say they were raised Christian but never went to church. Can you be Christian outside of a community of Christians?

Adam J. Copeland

Who is...
Adam J. Copeland

Church nerd alert: I served on the committee that developed a new Presbyterian hymnal!

The Christian faith is less about being a Christian than *living* and *loving* as one. Sure, one can call oneself a Christian and never go to church, but to do so is to miss the whole point of the faith. Christianity is more than getting a card punched and calling it good. Instead, Christians are to live lives worthy of our gifts and calling (Eph. 4:1–2).

It's no coincidence that most of the books in the New Testament are written to communities struggling with their faith and how to live together. Life in community is just plain hard sometimes. It's also difficult to live out one's Christian faith, whether alone or with others. (Which, in fact, is a reason Christians support one another in church and communities; they tackle the difficulty together.)

Beyond the basic challenge of Christian faith, the heart of the question gets at the larger cultural issue of individualism. So much of our culture tells us to live first and foremost for ourselves, but the Bible—and the message of Jesus— is almost always about life in relation to others.

When Western Christians read scripture texts, particularly Paul's letters, we usually assume any "you" in the letter is directed at an individual. In the original Greek, however, the vast majority of the time when we read Paul writing "you," he is addressing a group, a whole community. The "you" is most often a plural, as in "you all" (or "y'all" as they say in the South).

I suppose you can try to be a Christian alone, but I wouldn't recommend it. It might seem easy at first, but that's probably because it's not true Christianity.

Andrew Marin

A. What is a community? I irregularly went to church growing up and in my college years because of my sports schedule (I ended up playing Division I baseball on an athletic scholarship); and now I am hardly able to go to a church that I'm not speaking in because of my work travel schedule. Do those things prevent me from being a Christian?

I believe there is a strong undercurrent within contemporary Church culture that overemphasizes the physical "going to the building," and underemphasizes the power built in reading the Bible and talking to God—yes, talking to God and letting God talk back. The Reformation happened so that everyday people could get a Bible in their hands. That was done for a very good reason: *access*. So get a Bible, read it, learn from it, and let it inform and transform you. It's not just "pastors" who can tell you what is in the Bible and how it should affect your life.

Spiritual growth doesn't solely revolve around what happens inside the four walls of a building. (Sounds awfully similar to the Pharisees and their worship of the temple, doesn't it?) A church community is not a bad thing; it can give life, be an encouragement, and lend to sustainability of education and growth. I just ask that it be held in its proper proportion. When church and its inhabitants preach a message that church is the way to be a Christian, something has gone very wrong.

Phil Shepherd, *a.k.a.* The Whiskey Preacher

Who is...
Phil Shepherd

The majority of onomatopoetic words make my stomach queasy.

A. Closet space. I never thought I would be one of those people who coveted closet space. But I am now that person. Living in old homes with next-to-no closet space has made me a coveter, and I am not ashamed to say so. It's romantic to live in a space that has character and tradition, but most old homes lack closet and storage space. Clothes get piled in corners of rooms and the crockery gets placed in creative spaces that are sometimes not even in the kitchen. In the long run, even when you attempt to reduce the amount of stuff you have, the lack of closet space becomes confining, and you end up being a closet coveter like me.

Asking: "Can you be a Christian outside of a community of Christians?" reminds me of living in an old home, trying to put things in places where they don't necessarily fit because there's no room for where they are now. For many of us who grew up in church, having a system of categories of who's in, and who's out (Christian or non-Christian), was the only way we knew how to keep things organized and clean.

Romanticizing about clinging to the old ways has left no room for the changing world. I believe God is asking us to move into a place where there is more room so we don't have to ask who's in or out but instead live into the love that Jesus called *all* to live into.

Scriptural reference(s):

1 Corinthians 12:13–14
Ephesians 4:1–2

Suggested additional sources:

- *Let Your Life Speak* by Parker Palmer
- *Mere Churchianity* by Michael Spencer
- *Xealots* by Dave Gibbons
- HGTV
- *Church In the Inventive Age (Christianity Now)* by Doug Pagitt

Questions for further discussion/thought:

1. What do you like to do alone versus in community?
2. What do you like to do in community rather than by yourself?
3. What areas or topics are your local church not addressing, and how can you and a group of believers go about addressing them?
4. In an ever-changing culture, do Christian friends on Facebook and Twitter that you share intimate details with count as "community"?
5. Can we still be faithful to the gospel without having to ask who is in and who is out?
6. What does making room look like for the church?
7. If you are not a part of a faith community and yet you identify yourself as a Christian, what is keeping you from being a part of a faith community?

Source cited:

- *The Holy Bible*

When a baby is conceived, where do Christians believe that soul comes from? Is it created at that moment, or has it been floating in existence in the universe from the beginning of time?

Carol Howard Merritt

I was pregnant and exhausted. Extended puking had smattered my church business for months. I rarely took sick leave, but the fatigue overwhelmed me so that continuing my work felt like swimming laps in a pool of honey. I went home, collapsed on my bed, and immediately drifted to sleep.

The smell of vibrant flowers woke me. With my eyes wide open, the presence of the aroma was as real and strong as any bodily form.

I searched the room for flowers, potpourri, perfume, or any cause of the smell. I found nothing. So, I eased my bloated stomach back onto the bed. Rubbing my belly, I let the scent enrapture me and wondered if I somehow smelled the essence of my child. I had been a pastor long enough to hear stories of grieving loved ones who were visited by scents of those who passed. Could that smell be the soul of my unformed infant?

This experience compelled me to study what my tradition taught. Theologians call the notion that a soul exists before its present earthly body the "preexistence of souls." The idea became widespread with the Greek philosopher, Plato. Augustine of Hippo (whose writings helped form Western Christianity and influenced medieval philosophy) explored the possibility of a preexistence of souls, but ultimately rejected it. Most Christian thinkers have not held to the idea since Augustine, and there is no biblical evidence for it.

Personally, I believe that the body and soul are intimately connected and cannot be separated from one another. Yet, that afternoon still makes me wonder if I'm somehow wrong.

Christian Piatt

Who is...
Christian Piatt

The tendon in my left pinky finger is too short,
which makes my finger permanently crooked.

This assumes a relatively modern Western mindset that places the individual center stage. This has not always been the case. In fact, human beings were more community-minded for most of history, before the fierce individualism of today's world took hold. The ancient Jewish notion of sin wasn't so much focused on individual deeds as it was referring to the collective wellbeing and orientation of an entire group.

While mulling this idea over in bed at 2:00 in the morning, a quote from Louis CK's show, *Louie*, came to mind. In this particular scene, Louis CK is talking to a friend, Eddie (Doug Stanhope), who is contemplating suicide, and who is looking to CK for a reason not to follow through with his plan. Finally exasperated, CK hits him between the eyes with a profound truth:

"You know what," he says to Eddie, "it's not your life. It's *life*. Life is bigger than you, if you can imagine that. Life isn't something that you possess; it's something that you take part in, and you witness."

What if we don't each possess "a soul"? What if there is some greater "Collective Soul" (no, not the nineties garage band) in which we get to take part, but which we never own, so to speak?

The idea of a single, Collective Soul blows up the entire concept of personal salvation. There's no longer a possibility of individual salvation while others still suffer. Now, for some this might mean that the entire world has to be converted to Christianity before we can be truly reconciled with God. But I tend to think, based on Jesus' life and teaching, that it has more to do with lifting one another up and making ourselves collectively whole by working together toward the eradication of suffering—be it physical, emotional, or spiritual. In doing so, it's hard to imagine that I could sit back and consider my own personal salvation—however you interpret that—while others still suffer.

After all, their life is also my life.

Their soul is also my soul.

Their salvation is also my salvation.

It's not about you. It's not about me. It's about *us*.

Phil Snider

Who is...
Phil Snider

I will forever argue that Eddie Murray is the most underrated baseball player of my lifetime, and perhaps of all time.

Comedian and satirist Stephen Colbert once said that the soul is the result of a divine three-way, which I suppose is as good of an answer as there is. Those who definitively claim an answer to such questions are mostly guessing anyhow.

It's important to point out that biblical writers weren't so quick to differentiate between the "soul" and the "body" as this question might imply. For writers of the Hebrew Scriptures, humans don't possess a soul inasmuch as they are a soul. The soul is used in "reference to the whole person as the seat of desire and emotion, not to the 'inner self' as though this were something separate from one's being." The human person is an integrated whole; soul is "not a thing to have but a way to be."

From this perspective, the soul is constitutive of human life and vitality, not a separate substance that comes to (magically) attach itself to humanity, whether at conception or some other time. It's a way of referring to human being. This is why most modern-day English translations of the Bible often translate the Hebrew word for soul (*nefesh*) as "being" or "person": "[T]he Lord God formed man from the dust of the ground, and breathed into his nostrils the breath of life; and the man became a living being [*nefesh*]" (Gen. 2:7, NRSV). Translators don't want to lead us to believe that biblical writers understood the body and soul in dualistic terms, for this would be a misrepresentation of their worldview.

Doug Pagitt

This question asks us to think about our view of the cosmos. There are some who see the human body as a container in which the soul resides. But not me. I disagree with the suggestion that the body is matter and the soul is not. So, the question is raised: "When does this empty matter get real soul life?"

What we now know to be true is that matter and energy are not separate elements. We can now be holistic. Matter, at its core level, is made of atoms that are made of protons and electrons in dynamic movement; it only "appears" to be solid. All things are energy.

The spirit of someone is not separate from the body. We are not containers for our soul. We are whole beings, body, mind, and spirit. *Body* and *spirit* are one. So, we don't need to see the flesh as bad and spirit as good.

God is not only concerned with the nonmaterial. Since all things are energy, we need not make a distinction between soul and body, with one being of eternal value and the other of only earthly value.

Scriptural reference(s):

Genesis 2:7
Deuteronomy 6:5
1 Peter 2:6–16

Suggested additional sources:

- *Summa Theologiae* by Thomas Aquinas
- *On the Principles of Nature* by Thomas Aquinas
- *Mere Christianity* by C.S. Lewis
- "Soul," in *The New Interpreter's Dictionary of the Bible, Volume V*, by Joel B. Green

Questions for further discussion/thought:

1. What do you base your understanding of the human soul on? How does it affect your understanding of salvation?
2. Can a soul exist without a body? Why or why not?
3. When, why, and how do you believe a soul originates?
4. Why do you think Peter talked about the body making war against the soul? Do you think of the soul and body as two separate entities?
5. Do you think of the soul as something separate from the body?
6. When writers speak of the soul as the human seat of desire and emotion, does it help to interpret this from a poetic perspective? Do you think your interpretations would find resonance among the earliest biblical writers?

Sources cited:

- *Louie* (TV show) by Louis CK
- *The Confessions of Saint Augustine* by Augustine of Hippo, translated by R.S. Pine-Coffin (New York: Penguin Classics, 1961)
- "Preexistence of souls," *Essential Theological Terms* by Justo L. González (Louisville: Westminster John Knox, 2005)
- Phaedo: or, *The Immortality of the Soul* by Plato (public domain); can be downloaded on Kindle for free.
- "Saint Augustine," *Stanford Encyclopedia of Philosophy*, http://plato. stanford.edu/entries/augustine/
- "Soul," in *The New Interpreter's Dictionary of the Bible*, volume V, by Joel B. Green (Nashville: Abingdon, 2009)

It seems as if most Christians focus a lot more on issues of sex and sexuality than any other issue. Why?

Andrew Marin

The Church's pushback during the sexual revolution was to clearly instill the message that sex is a sacred gift of unity from God to be experienced with one's partner within a marriage context. This thought is the basis to why Christians are to wait to have sex until their wedding night. Though theologically correct, the Church has disproportionated this interpretation of love and sex as "the greatest gift God has given two people committed to each other for life." The problem, then, is that the past few generations of Christians have been proffered incorrect teachings and over-generalizations that have taken it one step further: sex is the greatest amount of love one can give to another.

The Bible says no such thing. What the Bible actually says is that the greatest expression of God's love to humanity is that God conforms us to the likeness of Christ. The Bible also says that the greatest expression of our love toward one another is to love God and love others like we have been first loved by God.

There is no hint of sex in any of those commands. Paul went so far to say that it is better to stay unmarried and serve God. However, if that is too difficult a task, it is then better to get married than to burn in hell with lust! In most scenarios the Church's overemphasis on sex is completely opposite to what the Bible actually teaches about love.

Brian Ammons

Who is...
Brian Ammons

I like squirrels.

On the one hand, I'm not sure I agree with the premise of the question. I think Christians talk around sex and sexuality a lot, but rarely get to talking about it directly. In fact, I think many Christians put a lot of energy into trying to avoid serious conversations about sex and sexual practice. I'm longing for some serious conversation about sex, about what works, why it's beautiful and sacred, and how to approach it as a form of prayer. I want to hear Christians talk about those things, but most of what I'm hearing are debates about who can do what with whom, and, if they are doing *that*, if they can then teach Sunday school. We make a mockery out of the sacred gift of sex.

On the other hand, it seems as if we live in a sex-saturated culture. It's not just Christians focusing on sex—it's the nightly news; it's prime-time television; it's the self-help industry. Part of why I wish Christians were really talking about sex is because so many of us are so hungry for a counter-narrative to the commodification of bodies and intimacy that we experience in the world. What would a sex-positive, Christian perspective based in spiritual practice look like?

So, while I am invested in continuing and promoting a conversation about sex and sexuality among Christians, I want a different one than the one that seems to be drawing our attention. I want that conversation to take its place alongside other spiritual practices and to find enough room for us to sit with our differences in the same way we do around how we baptize, worship, and pray.

Phil Jackson

For Christians, the issue of sex is often associated with shame, whether it is shame from personal history, family, or the abuse they see happening in their community. As Christians, the Bible teaches that we are to refrain from sex before marriage and that sex is for the marriage bed; but marriages, even Christian marriages, are falling apart all over the place. In addition, especially where I live and serve on the west side of Chicago, we have more baby mommas than wives, the highest rate of HIV among men and high STDs among youth and women. There is an urgency to prevent or stop all this pain; therefore, this bemoaning of inappropriate sexual behavior becomes a bandwagon issue for a lot of people to talk about. Yet why don't Christians talk about the other issues, such as what the circumstances are that cause people to have sex before marriage, or what part abuse plays in some of the promiscuity. The reason is because that would take a longer commitment, and perhaps involve walking with someone who is struggling. It might even expose the systems that cause the problems (which Christians or others may be benefitting from), thus causing those Christians to lose whatever benefits that system may have given them. The issues are hard and many, yet shining the light of Christ upon some of the darkest issues we face is exactly what Christ has called us to do.

Phil Shepherd, a.k.a. The Whiskey Preacher

I have this game I play with Stephanie, my wife—and, no, it's not *that* kind of game either (insert sly grin here). This game is an amalgamation of "Slug Bug" and "I Spy." While we're driving, every time I spot a Cadillac, I yell "Cadillac!" This annoys the hell out of Stephanie and, in reality, I am the only one really playing the "Cadillac" game. You see, I have always wanted to own a Cadillac. My father always wanted one, too, but my mother wouldn't let him have one. And my wife Stephanie thinks they are ugly and useless. "Our Toyota rides just as nice as a Cadillac," she has told me on more than one occasion. That's heresy at its finest, folks.

The more Stephanie tells me no, the more I talk about procuring a Cadillac by any means necessary (within the law…of course). Sex and sexuality, for many Christians, are like a Cadillac for me. If something is seen as unattainable or taboo, then it's human nature to obsess about what you can't have. At some point in our Western puritanical past, this idea materialized: if it was pleasurable, it equaled sinful. Sex became something you can't have, can't talk about. We have a legacy of trying to annex off our sexuality from our humanity, squashing this beautiful part of how we were created. I can't have a Cadillac; that becomes all I want to talk about. For Christians who haven't been free to talk about sex, now that's all they want to talk about.

Scriptural reference(s):

Genesis 2:24–25
Matthew 22:36–40
Romans 8:28–30
1 Corinthians 7:8–9
Hebrews 13:4

Suggested additional sources:

- *A Framework for Christian Sexual Ethics* by Margaret A Farley
- *Bringing Sex into Focus* by Caroline J. Simon (conservative)
- *God and Sex* by Michael Coogan
- *Real Sex* by Lauren F. Winner
- *Sex at Dawn* by Christopher Ryan and Cacilda Jetha (progressive)
- *Sexual Politics, Sexual Communities* by John D'Emilio (second edition)
- *The God of Sex* by Peter Jones
- *Sex and the Church* by Kathy Rudy
- *Body and Soul: Rethinking Sexuality as Justice-love* by M. Ellison and S. Thorson-Smith, eds.
- *The Ethics of Sex* by M.D. Jordan
- *A Loose Garment of Identifications* by Brian Ammons (2010), http://homebrewedchristianity.com/2011/03/02/thats-too-gay-brian-ammons-banned-chapter-from-baptimergent/
- *The Meaning of Sex* by Dennis Hollinger
- *Sex and Love in the Home* by David Matzo-McCarthy
- *The End of Sexual Identity* by Jennell Williams Paris

Questions for further discussion/thought:

1. What were you taught about sex growing up by your family and/or your church?
2. Does it differ from your understanding today, or what you will/might teach your own kids?
3. Do I see the gospel as holistic?
4. What are the issues I see that I don't get involved in and/or don't want to get involved in?
5. Have you compartmentalized your sexuality from your spirituality, and has that affected your overall life?

Source cited:

- *The Holy Bible*

Why does "living a Christian lifestyle" mean people quit drinking alcohol, or cussing, or watching R-rated movies, or listening to secular music?

Sean Gladding

Who is...
Sean Gladding

When I was 19, I pretended to be a Christian to get into Bible college.

We all have our moral scorecards (you don't recycle? really?), none more so than churches—especially churches where it's really important to be clear on who is "in" and who is "out." Sadly, most moral scorecards are of the negative variety, as the question notes. We know we are "good" Christians because of the things we *don't* do, or, perhaps more accurately, by the things people don't *see* us doing (perhaps why there are drive-up windows at the liquor store). Ask people what a Christian is, and increasingly the answer will be a list of things we are against.

I find this to be very sad, and it's one of the reasons I rarely self-identify as "Christian."

It's almost impossible not to see the irony of all this (although some of us are apparently determined not to). Taking a leap in the dark, I'm going to assume that a "Christian lifestyle" is one that looks somewhat like the life Jesus lived, as recorded in the four gospels. If we're going to define ourselves by what we are against, then let's do so by being against the things that Jesus was against, things such as hoarding wealth and possessions, or judging others, or taking revenge. Even better, perhaps we could express those positively. Thus, a "Christian lifestyle" becomes one in which we are *for* sharing our resources with those in need of them, accepting others, and nonviolence. Now that's a list I aspire to self-identify with.

Adam J. Copeland

I have a Christian friend who refuses to frequent any business that advertises itself as a Christian business. He avoids Christian car dealers, Christian counselors, and Christian nail salons. (OK, he avoids *all* nail salons, but you get the point.) My friend's boycott of businesses advertised as explicitly Christian is directly related to the fact that he can't stand self-righteousness. He abhors moralizing.

When people love God and profess Jesus Christ as Lord, they are compelled to respond in some way. Faith in Jesus changes lives, so it makes sense that those who claim their faith seek to live it out.

Some people approach this lived-out faith seeking a moral purity, confusing following Jesus with simple abstention. For them, faith simply equals not drinking or not cursing. I sympathize with the desire to clearly put one's faith into action.

Sure, it would be handy if we could measure faithfulness with a checklist of movies not to watch. It is tempting simply to label some things as Christian, and some not, and function with extremely clear boundaries. Perhaps some personalities are drawn to the black-and-white nature of such distinguishing lines. But absolutes can also stigmatize those who make other choices or who have different life experiences and boundaries.

My friend could certainly be criticized for his own rather rigid stance on avoiding "Christian" businesses. Maybe he is making a problematic lifestyle choice of a different nature. Perhaps he should check out that nail salon.

Phil Shepherd, *a.k.a.* The Whiskey Preacher

Who is...
Phil Shepherd

My cowboy boot size is a 13B.

Growing up with older brothers, I was taught at a very young age to be competitive: in sports, video games, Monopoly, or Risk. God forbid that you ever played against me! One of my friends would get so frustrated when playing Risk against me and my older brother Neal that he would leave after the game with a migraine headache and a bag of ice on his tensed-up neck. You could say my competitive nature is strong.

However, I pick my battles. I tend to shy away from endeavors I suck at, but I won't give up the fight easily. I am also a recovering fundamentalist. I tried to "live a Christian lifestyle," and I sucked at it. Being the competitor that I am, I gave it my damnedest, but I failed miserably. There was even a period when I tried to "fake it until I made it," but that didn't work out so hot for me either. Exhaustion set in and I got tired of not being me.

It was my youth pastor, Tracy, who showed me a healthier way to engage in my journey as a follower of God through the way of Jesus. Instead of trying to live by an unrealistic rubric of checklists, Tracy taught me about the greatest commandment: love the Creator and love the creation. The love of Christ freed me from a path of inward-focused self-destruction that many unfortunately call a "Christian lifestyle." It's much easier to live a checklist than to live a complex life of love.

Scriptural reference(s):

Matthew 5:38–42
Matthew 7:1–5
Matthew 22:36–40
Matthew 25:41–45
Romans 12:2

Suggested additional sources:

- *Stuff Christians Like* by Jon Acuff
- http://www.jonacuff.com/stuffchristianslike/
- *Living on Purpose* by Christine and Tom Sine

- *Right Here, Right Now* by Alan Hirsch and Lance Ford
- *An Emergent Manifesto of Hope* by Doug Pagitt and Tony Jones, eds.
- *The Practice of Love: Real Stories of Living into the Kingdom of God* by Jonathan Brink, ed.

Questions for further discussion/thought:

1. How would you define "living a Christian lifestyle"?
2. What are the helpful and problematic reasons for avoiding alcohol, cussing, R-rated movies, etc.?
3. Why do you think we make these kinds of lists?
4. What would you include in a list of what makes for a "Christian lifestyle"?
5. Have you ever lived your faith journey by a checklist?
6. What does it mean to you to live by the greatest commandment?

Source cited:

- Doug Pagitt is the first person I heard use the term, "Follower of God through the Way of Jesus."

I hear Christians say all the time that, good or bad, everything happens for a reason. What about genocide? Famine? Rape? What could the reason possibly be? Does there have to always be a reason?

Brian Ammons

I don't buy it. I understand that it is comforting how some people believe that the world is orderly and reasonable in some plan we can't understand. I find exactly the opposite to be true. If the deep suffering of genocide and rape is a part of God's plan, God seems to be pretty sadistic. What makes more sense to me is to believe that God is with us in our suffering—that, when all else has crumbled, we are not alone. While I resist the idea that God puts suffering into our lives for a purpose, I do believe that when we hold our pain loosely enough to invite God into it with us, it can be transformed and become purposeful.

The most concrete example of this in my own life is my experience as a survivor of childhood sexual violence. I do not hold God accountable for the choices that my abuser made. I tried that… It just left me angry and dead inside. But, as I've done work toward my own healing, I've been able to experience the journey that has come out of that abuse as full of grace and life. It's led me to work with young people, commit my life to engaging the church in complicated conversations, and deeply connect with vulnerable people. That's where God is for me. Not in the reason behind the suffering, but in the transformation of the suffering into hope. God is in the practice of resurrection.

Adam J. Copeland

Everything does happen for a reason, but let's not blame all the reasons on God. Just because an event is tragic does not mean God, with a conniving evil laugh, micromanaged the crisis from on high.

Take, for example, the fact that smoking cigarettes causes cancer. When a person who has smoked a pack a day for thirty years is diagnosed with cancer, there is "a reason" for the cancer. When a person with poor balance cleans the gutters, falls off a slippery roof, and breaks a leg, there is "a reason" for the broken bone. When a person drinks too much, then drives a car and causes a wreck, there is "a reason" for the incident.

The trick, in all these cases, is the right balance of noting the causes without blaming the person in need. We know that many cancers, household injuries, and car accidents are preventable, but that does not mean we should treat those affected with anything less than the utmost love and care.

Beyond these more clear reasons, however, I certainly admit that some events are so tragic, so dire, so horrifying that they defy all attempts at explanation. Indeed, in many cases even the most logical analysis of a tragedy's causes does not soothe one bit.

Ultimately, I cannot believe in a God who would engineer such tragedies as genocide, famine, and rape. I do believe, however, in a God who loves us through every trial and stays with us even to the deepest pit of despair.

Hugh Hollowell

Who is...
Hugh Hollowell

I co-parent four chickens.

Often, people who say things like that are people in pain who are searching for an explanation for things that otherwise make no sense, such as, to use your examples, rape or famine.

Sometimes bad things happen. In the Christian worldview, this is because we do not live in accordance with the plan God has for us. But regardless of why, sometimes bad things happen.

One helpful way to look at this is not that God causes these things to happen for a reason, but that God can use the bad things that do happen to accomplish good things such as the spirit of unity and love that came out of the tragedy of 9/11. God did not cause it, but God can use the bad things that happen to move God's dream for the world forward.

Margot Starbuck

Who is...
Margot Starbuck

*My childhood dream was to be a Solid
Gold dancer (not yet realized).*

It is human nature to prefer certainty over doubt or ambiguity. We'd rather be sure than unclear. We'd rather know than not know. Because uncertainty leaves room for anxiety to rise in our hearts, we'd much prefer to quell our fears, to soothe ourselves, with bold pronouncements of doctrinal certainty. "Everything happens for a reason" is one of those. I suspect it's this natural human temptation to relieve our own anxieties, rather than the revealed will or character of God, which causes us to make sweeping generalizations in an effort to explain what we don't understand.

Technically, of course, it is often true. One reason for genocide is the sinful segregation of peoples. A reason for famine is greed and inequitable distribution of resources. An explanation for rape is that a person who hurts deeply is someone who, himself, has been hurt deeply. Because there are twisted sinful reasons for human brokenness and depravity, however, does not make God the *author* of those reasons. In the release of God's people from captivity in Exodus, God is revealed as one who delivers threatened and oppressed people. In the wilderness, God provides for the hungry. In the person of Jesus, the bread of life, God feeds both souls and stomachs. In the Old Testament and again in the person of Jesus, God does not violate vulnerable women, but delivers and redeems them.

God is not a twisted dictator who inflicts suffering in order to teach people lessons. Though this interpretation may bring comfort or relief to some, it is a misrepresentation of the God who is revealed in the Scriptures as a redeemer and deliverer.

Scriptural reference(s):

Psalm 139
1 Corinthians 14:33
Ecclesiastes 3:1–8
James 1:13
1 John 1:5

Suggested additional sources:

- *Faith and Other Flat Tires: Searching for God on the Rough Road of Doubt* by Andrea Palpanat Dilly
- *Where Is God When Disaster Strikes?* (Adult Study) by Wendy Farley, The Thoughtful Christian, http://www.thethoughtfulchristian.com/Products/TC0067/where-is-god-when-disaster-strikes.aspx
- Read some Moltmann…any Moltmann
- Brian Ammons: http://homebrewedchristianity.com/2011/02/21/reframing-sexuality/
- http://www.ivpress.com/title/exc/1423-8e.php

Questions for further discussion/thought:

1. When have you felt these questions have been answered or not answered?
2. Does every situation need a reason?
3. What is the most troubling reality for you to reconcile with God's goodness and power?
4. Even if you believe that human suffering isn't authored by God, what sort of a letter of complaint might you like to address to the Almighty? (God can take it.)

What defines someone as an emergent Christian? Is it a worship style? A theology? What is it trying to achieve? Is there a difference between "emerging" and "emergent," or are they synonymous?

Phil Snider

A lot of variables are at play when it comes to understanding what has been described variously as emerging/emergent/emergence Christianity. For the most part, the early days of emerging Christianity (late 1990s–early 2000s) featured a lot of young evangelicals (or post-evangelicals) looking for an alternative to the Religious Right fundamentalism that dominated their childhood and youth. They began to engage more progressive approaches to Christianity that were sometimes outside of the conventional evangelical box. It didn't take long for critics to think they went too far. Many were accused of falling for the latest "liberal" or "postmodern" heresy. It became necessary, these critics thought, to distinguish between emerging and emergent Christians. Emerging Christians were designated as those seeking to reform evangelical practices in significant ways, but by maintaining the basic beliefs of evangelicalism. Those who challenged the belief system itself were deemed "emergent."

As time went by, Christian groups throughout the U.S. began to recognize that those identifying with emerging and/or emergent Christianity were actually part of a much larger conversation that aimed at figuring out what the church might look like in a postmodern culture (hence the shift in language to "emergence" Christianity). Nowadays, questions aren't so much about, "What is the emerging church and/or emerging worship?" but rather, "How does the church faithfully navigate the postmodern waters it finds itself in?" While nobody knows the answer, there is no shortage of folks trying to figure it out, whether they use language of emergence Christianity or not.

Carol Howard Merritt

Who is...
Carol Howard Merritt

I still fear being left behind in the Rapture.

I don't recognize the man, but I don't have to know him to realize he's disappointed by his surroundings: the choir, organ, robes, and pews. After the service, I track him down. Over hot tea, I find out he's on a pilgrimage of emergent churches. He attended Western Presbyterian, where I pastor, in the hopes of finding a hipster community with thrift-store couches, icons, and incense. Instead, he ended up in an intergenerational congregation, with traditional hymns, a one-way sermon, and by-the-book liturgy.

"I'm sorry," I say, although I'm not sure why. I don't have a particular duty to provide every worship tourist with a dose of emergent creativity. But the visitor (who also happens to be a pastor) read that I was a leader in the movement, so he came to Western. I know how rare free Sundays are for clergy, so I feel I've wasted something precious.

I also feel like a fraud. Again.

I'm recognized as an emergent leader because I write with a postmodern sensibility. I appreciate the power of narrative and question atonement theories. I'm a recovering Fundamentalist. I read Jacques Derrida, just for fun. I have dear friends in the movement. All of these are frequent symptoms of emergent Christianity.

But I feel outside of it. I chafe under emerging anti-denominational sentiments. When talking about gender within emergent circles, I often feel misunderstood. And I'm sure that any true emergent Christian would give me a good, old-fashioned eye rolling if I tried to explain the movement.

So I won't. I will simply state my own hope to stay open to the creative ways in which the Spirit is moving in a new generation.

Phil Shepherd, *a.k.a.* The Whiskey Preacher

I met Marilyn Manson once. We were both in the Denver airport waiting for our respective planes, and he was just sitting there reading his book and minding his own business. It took me by surprise that he was nothing like the media had portrayed him. He was soft-spoken, not flamboyant, nor was he sacrificing a goat over by the vending machines. He was not what I was expecting. Mind you, we are not best friends or anything, but I could tell he was a person of substance in the brief encounter we had.

I see the emergent church much like my encounter with Marilyn Manson, not exactly what folks are expecting. We like to nail things down. We like definitions so we can create a safe haven of certainty, where we can feel better about what is going on around us.

Emergent Christianity is not limited by definitions. It's not a specific worship style. It doesn't even adhere to one vein of theology. If it's trying to achieve one thing, it's conversation: a contextual/global conversation that is asking more questions than it seeks answers. Critics claim that this is a cop-out and that all the emergent church is trying to do is pervert the gospel with its ambiguities and the preaching of relative truth. My answer to those critiques is…maybe.

If I would call myself a Christian, I would call myself an emergent Christian, but that would be putting a label on it now…wouldn't it?

Scriptural reference(s):

The Book of Acts
1 Corinthians 12:12–27

Suggested additional sources:

- *A Generous Orthodoxy* by Brian McLaren
- *Reframing Hope: Vital Ministry in a New Generation* by Carol Howard Merritt
- *Emergent Manifesto of Hope* by Doug Pagitt and Dwight J. Friesen, eds.
- *The Great Emergence: How Christianity Is Changing and Why* by Phyllis Tickle
- *The New Christians: Dispatches on the Emergent Frontier* by Tony Jones
- *The Hyphenateds: How Emergence Christianity Is Re-Traditioning Mainline Practices* by Phil Snider, ed.
- www.emergentvillage.com
- www.transformnetwork.org
- www.knightopia.com
- www.postmodernegro.wordpress.com

Questions for further discussion/thought:

1. Do you sense any changes in American Christianity?
2. Generationally speaking, if the Builders worshiped in denominational church, and the Boomers created the evangelical mega-church, how

do you think Generation X and the Millennials will express their spiritual longings?

3. What excites you about the religious landscape in the United States? What makes you feel hopeful?
4. If you are part of a Christian community, how has it changed over the last ten to twenty years? Have the changes been for better or worse?
5. Should Christian churches always stay the same? Why or why not?
6. What dreams do you have for the future of the church?
7. How does your faith community contextually engage the larger community in which you live?
8. A big misnomer about the emergent church is that it is simply a new way to do social justice within the church. Do you believe that to be true, and, if not, how is it different?

Source cited:

• Jacques Derrida, *The Gift of Death* (Chicago: University of Chicago Press, 2007)

Carol Howard Merritt

A. "Can you see the Bible? Right there on that table," she pointed, without touching the precise oil brush strokes. "It's clear that our founders were God-fearing people."

My husband, Brian, and I squinted and nodded politely at the artist's rendering of a thick book. When the tour guide walked to the next work of art, I couldn't help but share a smile with Brian. It was our first time in our nation's capitol building and the third time we played "spot the Bible" in a painting.

We were guests of a family friend, a politician who rose to power during the Gingrich Revolution. Newt Gingrich armed the Religious Right for the Republican agenda. On this tour, every statue and painting had one point: it proved that the United States was a Christian nation. And the subtext followed: we Christians needed to take our nation back.

Yes, some people came to the United States with utopian visions of it being the "promised land." But we do not have a state-sanctioned church or a church-sanctioned state. We keep church and state separate. In recent decades, the Republican Party used "family value" issues, such as working against women's choice and same-sex rights, to keep conservative Christian Baby Boomers engaged, organized, and voting. The strategy will soon backfire, though, as younger Christians care more about starving people, ravaging wars, and environmental destruction than who's sleeping with whom.

Other Christians do not want the United States to become a theocracy. We want to make sure we maintain religious freedom for all Americans, whether they are Christians, Jews, Buddhists, Muslims, Hindu, Sikh, or none of the above.

Matthew Paul Turner

Who is...
Matthew Paul Turner

*I have an odd fascination for fiction
involving zombies and/or vampires.*

Not all Christians adhere to this understanding of American history. I don't, at least not anymore. But I do understand this type of thinking, since I was raised in a conservative Baptist church, one that adhered to the teaching that the United States was/is a "Christian nation." Some of the people at my church talked about the early settlers, the Pilgrims and Puritans who came to the New World for religious freedom, as if they were "New Israelites" or an updated version of "God's People" venturing into a God's new "promised land." John Winthrop once wrote that his hope was to make New England "as a city on a hill," a phrasing from the gospel of Matthew. Many Pilgrims/Puritans believed that their adventure was ordained by God to create a society that corrected all of the wrongs done by the Old World in the name of God.

This belief that the United States was/is a "Christian nation" is particularly important to America's brand of fundamentalism because it creates an easy-to-comprehend mental picture of a slope, one that they say showcases just how far the United States has slid down (and away) from the Puritanical ideals that this nation was "founded" upon, or the "Christian moral standards" it once valued. While it's true that many of our founding fathers viewed these ideas as an extension of their Christian faith, we also know that many others embraced these same ideas, not because of a great faith in God, but because they believed they were the good and right things to do.

Phil Jackson

Who is...
Phil Jackson

Love good music.

A. Hell no, we are not a Christian nation! In the same way that statement is an oxymoron, it is an oxymoron to say our country is a Christian nation. Just using the language of Christianity without being submitted to its purpose is hypocritical. However, it all depends upon your perspective of what you mean by a Christian nation.

Do you mean by Christian nation one that is founded by a group of leaders who started our country and lived double lives, only bringing God in when it was convenient, but keeping him in his little department the rest of their lives? Only bring him in when they needed to justify their actions? Keeping slaves as a way of life but not seeing them as humans created in the image of God, somehow omitting the slaves they owned from the equation when writing the founding documents of this country? If this is what is meant by a Christian nation, then I guess you're justified in calling it that.

Our political leaders use what is popular at the time to get the votes of the people, but to truly call ourselves a Christian nation means a lot more than what has been practiced. In some way America sought to give off an image that, because of the faith of our leaders, we would all fall in line with their faith. Constantine the Great was a Roman emperor from 306 to 337. Well known for being the first Roman emperor to convert to Christianity, Constantine and co-emperor Licinius proclaimed religious tolerance of all religions throughout the empire. People gave lip service to the emperor in order to win approval and gain some mobility or acceptance, but only a few were true to the faith. This history, perhaps, is where we get the idea of the America assumption of being a Christian nation, yet it crushed all that were pure about the faith. If we were seeking to live out, as a nation, what Jesus taught—that blessed are those who are the peacemakers for they will be called sons of God, or blessed are the meek for they shall inherit the earth—we would look and live a lot different.

Scriptural reference(s):

Matthew 5:1–12

Suggested additional sources:

- *Raised Right: How I Untangled My Faith from Politics* by Alisa Harris
- *Crazy for God: How I Grew Up as One of the Elect, Helped Found the Religious Right, and Lived to Take It All (or Almost All) of It Back* by Frank Schaeffer
- "Alisa Harris and Raised Right," *God Complex Radio* by Derrick Weston, http://godcomplexradio.com/2011/11/gcr-5-4-alisa-harris-and-raised-right/
- *The History of the Church: From Christ to Constantine* by Eusebius (author), Andrew Louth (ed., Introduction), G. A. Williamson (trans.)

Questions for further discussion/thought:

1. Does your faith inform your activism? Do politics inform your faith?
2. Do you think there is a problem with Christianity being so closely identified with the Religious Right?
3. What sort of problems do churches face when they allow a political party to set their agenda?
4. Do Christian principals cover all people equally?
5. Who should determine the interpretation of Christian principals if a nation sought to engage someone for that purpose?

Sources cited:

- *Utopia: The Search for the Ideal Society in the Western World* by The New York Public Library (Cambridge: Oxford University Press, 2001)
- *The History of the Church: From Christ to Constantine* by Eusebius (author), Andrew Louth (ed., Introduction), G. A. Williamson (trans.)
- "A Model of Christian Charity," a sermon by John Winthrop, 1630. available on many websites

How is it that so many Christians support, or even call for, wars when one of the names for the Christ they supposedly follow is "Prince of Peace," and Jesus urged love for enemies and nonviolent responses?

Carol Howard Merritt

The issue of war is complicated, both in our Scriptures and our tradition. The Old Testament is fraught with horrific stories in which God calls for the complete annihilation of men, women, and children. Jesus was called the Prince of Peace, but even Jesus said perplexing things such as, "Do not think that I have come to bring peace to the earth; I have not come to bring peace, but a sword" (Mt. 10:34, NRSV). Many followers expected Jesus to triumph over the oppressive Roman government, but Rome crucified him instead.

Our Christian tradition varies widely. While strong pacifist thought flows throughout Christianity, many Christians held tightly to the Just War Theories of Augustine of Hippo and Thomas Aquinas. They stated that war could be waged if there was a just cause, a properly instituted authority waged the war, and peace was the central motive in the midst of violence.

Of course, Augustine was writing during the fourth and fifth century when no one could imagine nuclear annihilation. No one could foresee that the United States would spend more on its military than the rest of the world combined. No one could dream of the barbarism that the richest country in the world could accomplish in strip bombing the poorest countries. No one could imagine how one nation could be so powerful that they could fight two wars without having hardly any impact on its citizenry. There is no way to compare the Old Testament annihilation of a fortified village or what Augustine described with the destruction we now accomplish with the press of a button.

American Christians need to struggle long and hard before they imagine any war that we pursue as just.

Christian Piatt

In his book, *Jesus and Nonviolence: A Third Way*, Walter Wink dismantles the myth that Jesus was a pacifist. Far from it, actually. Things like turning the other cheek and walking the second mile, in the context of Wink's nonviolent activist engagement, take on unexpected power, much like a black belt in aikido uses the energy of his attacker to overthrow him.

The great deception, says Wink, is that we Western-minded folks have bought the idea that we have two choices when faced with violence, injustice, or oppression: fight back in kind or do nothing. What is required, he says, is a third option, as modeled by Jesus, one that too often Christians and other people of faith mistake as a call for non-involvement.

As Wink claims, doing nothing in response to injustice is to implicitly support the violence already being done. But by acting in kind toward our enemy, we perpetuate the violence, becoming no better in many ways than the wrong to which we are responding.

Wink also effectively dispels the myth that violence, in any instance, has ever been a more effective tool than a nonviolent response. Ultimately more blood is shed and more people die, even if it's in our nature to want an eye for an eye.

Many of us can't think of the way Wink understands the teaching and life of Jesus as really a possibility for us. But, ultimately, it depends on how you measure success. If we consider the end of Jesus' ministry to be his moment of crucifixion—alone, vulnerable, and betrayed by those he continued to love—then his life's mission was a failure.

If, however, we believe that one life—perhaps even our own—is worth giving up for a change that brings hope to thousands or millions of others, many of whom we may never meet, then this third way begins to look like a path worth exploring and trying to imagine.

Two Friars and a Fool

God abhors violence. Human cruelty is the reason God repents of creation in the story of the flood. The law Israel receives from God on Mt. Sinai is replete with statutes designed to limit violence and urge mercy toward outsiders.

The prophets Isaiah and Jeremiah counseled total disarmament in the face of invasions by Assyria and Babylon, saying that their only security lay in God. Micah looked forward to the reign of God's Shalom as a time when the world would turn implements of war into tools of production, and no one would learn war anymore.

Jesus rejected multiple opportunities to be a militant messiah, commanded his disciples to put away their swords, and forgave his murderers while they were still in the act of executing him. When Jesus returned triumphant, he did not whisper a word of retribution against Rome, but offered further forgiveness to the disciples who had betrayed him and told them to take his peace into all the world. His earliest followers universally eschewed any form of violence, choosing martyrdom by the hundreds rather than pick up a sword in self-defense.

Paul, a violent zealot before Jesus found him, was one of those martyrs. He died proclaiming that we share Christ's ministry of reconciliation, that God is abolishing all divisions between people, and that our only enemies are spiritual ones.

We cannot carry both a cross and a sword. A person can either follow Christ or engage in violence, but not both at the same time.

Scriptural reference(s):

Genesis 6:9–13
Exodus 21:1–27
Leviticus 19:17–18; 24:19–22
Deuteronomy 19:1–7
Isaiah 11:1–10, 36–39, 65:17–25
Jeremiah 21
Micah 4
Matthew 4:1–11; 5:38-40; 10:34; 26:52; 28:19
Luke 4:1–13; 6:27–36; 22:36; 23:34
John 18:11; 20:19–23; 21:15–19
Acts 7:54–60; 9:1–19
2 Corinthians 5:18–21
Galatians 3:28
Ephesians 6:12
Revelation 21

Suggested additional sources:

- *Jesus and Nonviolence: A Third Way* by Walter Wink
- http://gandhifoundation.org/resources/
- *The Autobiography of Martin Luther King, Jr.* by Martin Luther King Jr., Clayborne Carson, ed.
- *The Hunger Games Trilogy* by Suzanne Collins
- *War Is a Force That Gives Us Meaning* by Christopher Hedges
- *Readings in Christian Ethics: A Historical Sourcebook* by J. Philip Wogaman and Douglas M. Strong, eds.

- *The Politics of Jesus* by John Howard Yoder
- *The Powers that Be* by Walter Wink
- *The Power of Non-violence* by Martin Luther King Jr.

Questions for further discussion/thought:

1. Was Jesus a pacifist? Did he ever justify or demonstrate the use of violence?
2. How do you understand the Christian response to injustice, violence, or oppression?
3. Is there ever justification within the context of the Christian faith to respond to any situation with violence?
4. What are your personal memories of war?
5. What do you know about the many wars of the last thirty years? Can you name them all?
6. Do you hold to a Just War theory? Are you a pacifist? What do you think about war?
7. Jesus said, "Blessed are the peacemakers, for they shall be called children of God" (Mt. 5:9, NRSV). What does it mean to be a peacemaker in your context?
8. Whether you agree with the above or not, what do you think of people who identify as Christian but serve in the military or the police, where they carry weapons and may be called upon to kill someone? What do you think Jesus would say to people serving in the military or police forces in your country?
9. Is there a situation in which you could imagine yourself killing another human being? Why or why not?

Source cited:

- *Jesus and Nonviolence: A Third Way* by Walter Wink (Minneapolis: Fortress, 2003)

Does somebody have to believe in the literal Resurrection in order to be a Christian?

Adam J. Copeland

Who is...
Adam J. Copeland

At 28, I retired from running marathons. I ran two—painfully.

In my denomination, the Presbyterian Church (USA), there is a long history of arguing over "the essential tenants" of faith. To summarize a few hundred years of history in a sentence: we largely agree that there must be essentials of the faith; we just can't seem to agree what they are.

For many (actually, for the *vast majority* of Presbyterians), if they were asked to compose a list of the essential faith tenants, belief in the literal bodily Resurrection of Jesus would likely make the cut. But, such lists are dangerous, for they miss the point.

Boiling down faith in Jesus Christ, God's son crucified and risen, to a mere checklist of doctrines cheapens the faith. Too easily such pursuits become fixated on angels dancing on pinheads instead of vital heartfelt faith that welcomes seasons of questioning and doubt and responds to God's love for the world.

Each of the four gospels tells of Jesus' death and the miraculous good news of his Resurrection (though each in a slightly different way). Before the gospel writers get to the cross, though, they tell of Jesus' encounters with believers. Jesus' ministry was less about defining essential tenants than pushing believers to a renewed, deeper understanding of the faith they already had.

Doug Pagitt

Who is...
Doug Pagitt

I hate lists of interesting things about me.

No. There is nothing someone has to believe to be Christian. Christianity is not based on right belief.

If you put all the things in the 2000 years of Christianity that the differing groups have had on the "have to believe" list, there would be no topic that makes it on all the lists.

It is a myth that there is a generic Christianity that all people have held to. One tradition's requirement is another tradition's nonessential. That doesn't mean there are not beliefs that each tradition requires for admittance to their group, but there are faithful Christians who differ on every topic, especially when the requirement uses a qualifying term like "literal." Every time an adjective is used, the disagreements increase. Some will say you need to believe in resurrection. Then someone else will qualify what kind of resurrection with the term "literal." That is a way of tightening the meaning.

This is not to say that people don't have beliefs or that beliefs don't matter. It is to suggest that our beliefs are changeable, adaptable, qualifiable. While powerful, they are not good when used as restrictions.

Hugh Hollowell

If by literal, you mean, "Jesus walked out of that tomb, and if I had been there with a video recorder, I could have recorded it," then, no, I don't think so.

It is not clear that even the apostle Paul understood it that way (see, for example, 1 Corinthians 15:35–50, in which he seems to say we will shed our human body and put on a spiritual body) , and we have no clue what the other early Christians thought happened. The writings describing it did not show up until about thirty years later, and the original text of the Gospel of Mark, the first Gospel to be written, seems unaware there even was a resurrection.

So no, I don't think you do. However, Most Christians throughout history have subscribed to some form of resurrection belief, whether it was the earthly/spiritual body Paul describes in 1 Corinthians 15, or a spiritual resurrection of sorts, or full-blown zombie Jesus, walking around in the same body he was killed in.

Scriptural reference(s):

Mark 9:24
James 2:14–17

Suggested additional source:

- *Reading the Bible Again for the First Time* by Marcus Borg

Question for further discussion/thought:

1. Are there some aspects of faith that really must be essential?

Why do Christians focus on the Ten Commandments but not any of the other laws found in the Old Testament, such as those found in Leviticus?

Adam J. Copeland

Of all the laws in the Old Testament, only the Ten Command-ments are spoken directly by God. They appear twice, first in Exodus 20:2–17, and then later Moses recalls them in Deuteronomy 5:5–21. In context, the Ten Commandments are tied to the larger story of God rescuing the Israelites out of Egypt and leading them to the promised land. As William Brown puts it, "As God *delivered* a people, so God *delivered* the commandments."

But even as important as the Ten Commandments remain, Jesus himself summarized the law in a much shorter fashion. When asked which command-ment was the greatest, Jesus said, "You shall love the Lord your God with all your heart, and with all your soul, and with all your mind." He then offered a second commandment, similar to the first: "You shall love your neighbor as yourself" (Mt. 22:37, 39, NRSV).

In the Gospel of John, Jesus also gives the disciples a new commandment: "that you love one another. Just as I have loved you, you also should love one another" (Jn. 13:34, NRSV).

Jesus was a good Jew who sought to keep God's commandments. Yet, Jesus also summarized and explained the goal of the commandments, framing them in love of God and neighbor. Contemporary Christians emphasize Jesus' interpretations rather than following all 613 laws found in the Old Testament. After all, *Ten* Commandments are hard enough to remember.

Hugh Hollowell

The cynic in me would say it is probably because we like wearing poly-cotton blend shirts and eating shrimp, two things prohibited in Leviticus that most Christians have no problem with today.

A more serious answer is that the Ten Commandments are an enumer-ated list of do's and don'ts, and we like lists, as long as they are not too long. And, more important to the Christian way of thinking, they are a list that does not contradict any of the teachings of Jesus, whom Christians believe to be the final revelation of God, or the practices or beliefs of the early church. The same is not true of the dietary restrictions or many of the ceremonial acts described elsewhere in the Hebrew Scriptures.

See, most Christians believe that Jesus made most of those things unnecessary, so they ignore them. But it is always a good idea to not kill people or to not want what belongs to others, so we kept those around.

Sean Gladding

Who is...
Sean Gladding

I am a massive fan of the new Doctor Who.

Pop quiz: which was a recent headline in my local newspaper?

A. *"Ten Commandments Fight is Costly"*
B. *"Local Farmer Fined: Reaped to the Corners of His Field"*
C. *"Man Accused of Raising Rabbits for Food"*

If you answered "A," you win a Moses action figure with detachable stone tablets! If you answered "B" or "C," you obviously have been reading Leviticus recently.

Judging by media coverage, it would indeed appear that Christians are willing to go to great expense to post the Ten Commandments in public places, but not so much for posters about, say, leprosy. As the question asks, "Why?"

Clearly the Ten Commandments are a weighty cultural icon in the United States, either as a set of rules that *those* people ought to keep, or that *those* people should stop shoving down our throats. Perhaps the reason they gain so much attention among Christians is because between the first word, "God," and the last word, "neighbor," lies the core content of the Great Commandment, to love God and to love neighbor. I suspect, however, the drive to display them publicly comes from the sense that we have lost our way as a society. Pick up any local newspaper and read what we do to one another, and I understand why some Christians want to have something concrete to point at and say, "This is how we should treat one another." This probably does not include Leviticus's concerns about the color of hairs growing out of skin blemishes.

Now, whether or not those same Christians take the Ten Commandments as seriously as they say they do is another question.

Scriptural reference(s):

Exodus 20:1–17
Leviticus 11:6
Leviticus 13:29–33
Leviticus 19:9
Deuteronomy 5:5–21
Matthew 22:34–40
John 13:34
Romans 13:8–10

Suggested additional sources:

* *The Ten Commandments* by David Hazony
* *Losing Moses on the Freeway* by Chris Hedges
* *Interpretation: The Ten Commandments* by Patrick Miller
* http://www.youtube.com/watch?v=wiWLCO_nMk0

Questions for further discussion/thought:

1. What commandments are the most important in your mind?
2. How many of the Ten Commandments can you name, without looking?
3. What has been your experience with the Ten Commandments, and how has that shaped how you think about them?

Source cited:

* *The Ten Commandments: The Reciprocity of Faithfulness* by William P. Brown (Louisville: Westminster John Knox Press, 2004), p. 2

Carol Howard Merritt

Who is...
Carol Howard Merritt

I read Manga.

A. "You shall not kill" is a simple command that Christians recognize, but how it affects our beliefs and behaviors can be surprisingly complicated. There doesn't seem to be much logical consistency to the notion that life is so important that a fetus ought to be protected from the moment of conception, but anyone should have the right to bear arms and crimes ought to be punishable by death.

From a biblical perspective, Old Testament laws treat ending a pregnancy (even when it's ended as an act of violence) as much different than murder. And "turn the other cheek" doesn't seem compatible with most NRA slogans. Of course, we have seen so many questionable death penalty verdicts, particularly against poor or underrepresented racial ethnic communities, that any Christian ought to shudder at the thought. Even without judicial system bias, does the death penalty make sense in the light of "love your enemies"?

Of course, this logic doesn't have as much to do with Christianity as it does with something closely related to Christianity: patriarchy. The patriarchal model works when men make the decisions for women. The male will, in return, provide for and protect the female and her offspring. We have many rituals of patriarchy (such as the father "giving" his daughter to be married), and its logic often permeates our society, often without question.

Pro-choice advocates want to take away the decision-making from men and give women the choice. If gun rights and the death penalty are taken away, then that lessens the ability for a man to protect his family. In both situations, patriarchy would be endangered.

Phil Snider

I've always respected the ethical consistency of those who advocate for a seamless garment of life, i.e., those who are pro-life across the board, including opposition to war and the death penalty. Inasmuch as 250 words allow, this reflects the position I hold today (if I had more words I'd add a few nuances).

In order to make sense of the incongruities harbored in this question, theorists point out that some who support things like the death penalty or war yet oppose abortion do so because unborn babies are innocent, whereas those sentenced to the death penalty, or those who are victims of war, are not innocent. Yet even this line of thought fails to recognize that no small percentage of those on death row are wrongly accused, and that the number of civilians killed in war often exceeds the number of soldiers killed, all of which should give us pause.

Moreover, any ethic that claims to be pro-life must be concerned about caring for babies even, and especially, after they are born. Numerous studies show that if a society truly wants to reduce the number of abortions, then reducing the rate of poverty is essential. It's hypocritical, as John Caputo notes, "to populate the killing fields of poverty by aligning oneself with, or even remaining silent about, policies that exacerbate economic and social injustice, which seed and cultivate the fields of abortion... [T]he right to life spans the entire spectrum and it includes not only fetuses but felons, not only friends but enemies, 'from womb to tomb.'"

Sean Gladding

This question describes the views of some of my friends who see themselves as being "pro-life," a position which I suspect the questioner in this case would see as being problematic. Here is how they have explained their views to me. God is the giver of life, and we are called to protect human life, especially that of those who cannot protect themselves, most obviously the unborn. Hence, owning and being willing to use a weapon to defend human life is consistent with being pro-life, even if the aggressor is killed in the process. The death penalty for murder is, in their opinion, both sanctioned by scripture and is the ultimate expression of belief in the sanctity of human life. They see these beliefs as being consistently pro-life, which is the point at which I disagree.

Regardless of whether we believe the death penalty as it is practiced in the U.S. is a deterrent against murder (it is not), or is applied justly (it is not), every time we take a life, we are enacting the belief that this person's life is irredeemable, that forgiveness and reconciliation are impossible, and/or that this life is less valuable than others, all of which deny the power and work of Christ, who, lest we forget, was himself executed by the State. If we are going to be against abortion, let us also be pro-life following birth, striving to provide for all children the abundant life Jesus promised.

Scriptural reference(s):

Genesis 9:6
Exodus 20:1–17
Exodus 21:12
Exodus 21:22–25
Matthew 5:39–46
Romans 13:1–4

Suggested additional sources:

- *Whose Freedom? The Battle over American's Most Important Idea* by George Lakoff
- *The Political Mind: A Cognitive Scientist's Guide to Your Brain and Its Politics* by George Lakoff
- *God's Politics: Why the Right Gets It Wrong and the Left Doesn't Get It* by Jim Wallis
- *The Death Penalty Debate* by H. Wayne House and John Howard Yoder
- http://www.amnesty.org/en/death-penalty
- *Dead Man Walking*, movie

Questions for further discussion/thought:

1. What do you think about abortion, the death penalty, and gun laws?
2. Do you think that the particular stances that some Christians take have more to do with politics, patriarchy, or the Bible?
3. According to studies, you are far more likely to be killed by a gun if you own a gun. Why do you think this is the case?
4. What does "pro-life" mean for you? How did you come to that understanding?
5. Do you have friends who think differently than you about this? How can you engage in constructive conversation with each other?

Source cited:

- *What Would Jesus Deconstruct?* by John Caputo (Grand Rapids, Mich.: Baker Academic, 2007)

Question

Many Christians describe themselves as "evangelical." What does that mean? Is that the same as being conservative?

Andrew Marin

Who is...
Andrew Marin

I received a Division I athletic scholarship to play baseball in college and was teammates with New York Yankees All-Star centerfielder Curtis Granderson.

A. I consider myself an evangelical. The problem with that word is a vocal cross-section of self-proclaiming evangelicals who see it as their only job to make others have "correct" theological and political beliefs. This has led to the confusion of the definition.

I believe reclaiming the word *evangelical* starts with how Christians view their call by Jesus in Matthew 28 as the Great Commission. Living in the Great Commission doesn't mean it will ever turn into the Great Reality. There will always be an "other," an opposite—those who will never believe, be on our side, or agree with who we are, and what we're all about. OK. Now that we've got that out of the way, the main question is: What do we do with "those" people? The answer should be the job of the evangelical. Here is my brief starting point:

The struggle for any label is both clumsy and backward because inherent to labels are issues of branding, access, and the potential privilege that comes with "correct" associations with said label. I am Andrew, a man who loves progressives and conservatives and works with both while faithfully seeking to establish the Kingdom here on earth as it is in heaven. What happens from that work of faithfulness is not my business. Rather, it is a challenge to me to see if I actually do believe what the Bible says, that it's the Holy Spirit's job to convict, God's job to judge, and mine to love.

Carol Howard Merritt: About twenty years ago, I was a conservative Christian. (Since then, my views have changed.) We called ourselves "fundamentalists" and were proud that we held to the five fundamentals of the faith (six-day creation, virgin birth, substitutionary atonement, Christ's divinity, and hell). Soon historians like Martin E. Marty and Scott Appleby began to link the word "fundamentalism" to Jewish and Muslim people.

Fundamentalism quickly dropped out of favor as a term, but the litmus test of belief still remains strong.

When Charismatic, nondenominational, and Bible-believing Baptist congregations became more organized in their political action, they needed a label to express to the media, donors, and politicians who they were and how their constituents represented a growing force. "Evangelical" fit nicely. It was a historic word and it has two Greek roots meaning "good" and "messenger," so it highlights the importance of spreading the gospel. People like Jerry Falwell could suddenly get face time on CNN, not because he was the founder of a small Christian college, but because he spoke for millions, he spoke for the "Evangelicals."

Now sociologists label people in terms of "evangelical" in order to designate conservative Christian groups. But most labels get muddy as they try to tidy up a messy reality. "Evangelical" also has historic resonance for many in liberal denominational churches; in fact, one of the major progressive denominations is the Evangelical Lutherans. Many people in historically liberal denominations consider themselves to be evangelical. And there are many liberal or progressive Christians who are also evangelical.

Matthew Paul Turner

A. When I was in my twenties, a very gentle pastor taught me that "to be an evangelical" means "you're a follower of Jesus, one who embraces the teachings of Christ, one who engages God through Jesus and community." He also taught me that to be "evangelical" means that you are one who pursues loving the poor, showing compassion to widows, and believing that the last truly are the first.

But his definition did not match the one I heard Christians and non-Christians in media use. They downsized the definition to reflect people who were "conservative" or "biblical" in their views on politics, social issues, and morality. Rarely was Jesus mentioned.

In 2006, I called that old pastor friend of mine to ask a question. "Does 'being evangelical' mean that I have to also be a conservative?" I said.

He laughed. "Who the hell told you that? Being evangelical means you're kind, compassionate, and hope-filled. You can do that and be conservative or liberal."

So, as self-proclaiming evangelical, I don't believe that "evangelical" is a synonym for "conservative." For me, it means I am passionate about the things of Jesus, knowing those things, doing those things, hoping those things, and trying my best to live those things.

Scriptural reference(s):

Matthew 22:36–40
Acts 17:11
Romans 14:10–12

Suggested additional sources:

- *The King Jesus Gospel* by Scot McKnight
- *With* by Skye Jethani
- *The Reason for God* by Timothy Keller
- *Fundamentalisms Observed* by Martin E. Marty and R. Scott Appleby
- *The Fall of the Evangelical Nation* by Christine Wicker

Questions for further discussion/thought:

1. Do you know "evangelicals" who look, think, and act differently? What draws you to each?
2. Do you think Jesus would have labeled himself as an evangelical?
3. How do you understand the term "evangelical"?
4. Do you think of the term in a historic, theological, or political sense?
5. Once politicians and the larger society adopt a term, do you believe that the historic sense can still apply, or does it lose its meaning?

Source cited:

- *What Is an Evangelical?* by Andrew Marin, (http://sojo.net/blogs/2011/10/24/andrew-marin-answers-what-evangelical)

What's different about postmodern Christianity? I hear the word postmodern used a lot among Christians, especially younger ones, but it's not clear what is meant by it.

Phil Shepherd, *a.k.a.* The Whiskey Preacher

Who is...
Phil Shepherd

I love to eat hominy.

A. Remember those pictures-hidden-within-pictures from the mid-90s? If you stared at them long enough and relaxed your eyes, the image would pop out at you. In the cult classic movie *Mallrats*, the character William spent the majority of the movie trying to make the picture reveal itself to him. Everyone around him could see it, but he never could see it himself.

When I think about postmodernity, I think about those pictures. Postmodernity has to do with how we see things. Postmodernity is a worldview shift, from modernity to postmodernity. One view is not better or worse than the other, they're just different. Modernity is based on quantifiable facts and concrete truths, trying to explain everything, whereas postmodernity views the world through experience and sees conclusions as relative, leaving room for mystery—the unexplained. Neither one is better than the other; they're just different.

Postmodern Christianity is often connected to younger Christians who've embraced this worldview shift, either because they never looked at the world through another lens, or, if they did, they realized the modern lens they were looking through looked out of focus to them. Postmodernity is mistakenly seen as a generational worldview, but I would strongly disagree. My mom, who turned seventy this past summer, views the world through a postmodern lens as much (if not more so) than I do, which I find fascinating. She embraces the idea that not everything in the world needs to be explained, especially God.

Phil Snider

Who is...
Phil Snider

The only time I've ever truly been proud of accomplishing something musically—I can't carry a tune for the life of me—was when I learned to play Simon and Garfunkel's "Bookends" on acoustic guitar.

For most of Western history, Christians understood God as a supernatural Supreme Being, a somewhat benevolent "Zeus" reigning from on high, or at least an Ordering Cosmic Presence that distinguished Right from Wrong.

During the period of the Enlightenment (what historians refer to as "modernity"), lots of people became suspicious of supernatural images of God. Rationalism trumped superstition. Modern philosophers argued that the emphasis of Christianity shouldn't be on a Big Strong Super Being who can divinely intervene on a whim, but rather on ethics. This is why Thomas Jefferson famously cut out all the miracle stories in the New Testament but kept the ethical teachings of Jesus.

Yet Nietzsche (like Debbie Downer from Saturday Night Live) stepped onto the scene and said ethics were mostly the conventions of society, not universal, metaphysical truths as the philosophers led us to believe. Religion was caught in a bind: if superstitious beliefs about God no longer held, and our ethical practices simply reflected the conventions of dominant culture, then there wasn't much use for religion. For all practical purposes, God was *dead*.

But just when it appeared Nietzsche had driven home the final nail in God's coffin, postmodern philosophers challenged us to reassess the role of religion. Several postmodern theorists concede there may not be a Supreme Being or Presence "out there," yet they point out how our hearts are hungry for all that is evoked in the name of God to come true (love, justice, etc.). We are hungry for love to be actualized, for justice to be done, and every time we try to adequately name what we mean by love or justice, all our words come up short. What we hope and long for exceeds all our ready-made concepts, whether we call such excess "God" or not. And even though love is never fully actualized and justice is never fully done, the desire for all that is stirring in the name of love or justice (or in the name of God) is precisely what puts us in its tracks. Here we step foot on postmodern religious ground, believers and atheists alike.

Andrew Marin

Leading progressive theologian Dr. Tony Jones asserts that postmodernism, in general, is not relativism or skepticism, but rather paying close attention to (1) details, (2) a sense for the complexity and multiplicity of things, (3) close readings, (4) detailed histories, and (5) sensitivity for differences. Thus, I see postmodern Christianity as the boldness to question the traditional hierarchies, fields of knowledge, and mediums of engagement that have been blindly taken as truth and gospel for the sole reason that the dominant majority purports them as the only acceptable way of belief and conduct.

This questioning does not infer there must be a wholesale drop of absolute truth, whether in Scripture or tradition. It does mean that there has to be an ability to freely think, feel, and question even the smallest aspects of the faith. As culture continues to shift, so must the contextualization of how to relate to and present Scripture and the principles of Jesus in meaningful ways that compel others to believe and act.

Scriptural reference(s):

Psalm 63:1

Suggested additional sources:

- *Everything Must Change* by Brian McLaren
- *Jesus for President* by Shane Claiborne and Chris Haw
- *The Sacredness of Questioning Everything* by David Dark
- *Who's Afraid of Postmodernism? Taking Derrida, Lyotard, and Foucault to Church* by James K. A. Smith
- *What Would Jesus Deconstruct? The Good News of Postmodernism for the Church* by John Caputo
- *On Religion* by John Caputo
- *God, the Gift, and Postmodernism* by John Caputo and Michael Scanlon, eds.
- *How (Not) to Speak of God* by Peter Rollins
- *The Divine Conspiracy: Rediscovering Our Hidden Life In God* by Dallas Willard

Questions for further discussion/thought:

1. In your life, do you see any distinctions that you inherently question from previous generations?

2. What are times when your questioning led you to change your belief, and times when your questioning led you to keep your same belief?

3. Augustine of Hippo once asked the question: "What do I love when I say I love my God?" Here he acknowledged that even though he felt called by something, even though he felt a claim upon his life, he was never quite sure who or what was doing the calling. That which grasped him always remained beyond his grasp. (This is why he also said, "If you comprehend it, it is not God.") Do you ever feel grasped by something that is beyond your grasp, something that you can't quite put words to? Have you ever thought about such an experience in religious terms?

4. What lens do you see the world through?

5. What fears, if you have any, do you have concerning the shift from modernity to postmodernity?

6. How do you think the church has been affected by the advent of postmodernity?

Sources cited:

- *The New Christians: Dispatches from the Emergent Frontier* by Tony Jones (San Francisco: Jossey-Bass, 2008)
- *Mallrats*, directed by Kevin Smith, Rouge Pictures, 1995

What do Christians believe about the nature of God? Do they believe that God is a transcendent "Other" that sits out there beyond this reality? If so, does God bridge the gap to deal with human affairs? Can we bridge the gap to reach God? Or is God not a transcendent Other but a part of us? Or some middle ground, something else altogether? Are we a part of God?

Carol Howard Merritt

Who is...
Carol Howard Merritt

I wanted to be Amy Grant.

Christians hold to a spectrum of beliefs when it comes to God's relationship with humanity. Some are functional deists, and believe that God is transcendent and leaves us to our own devices. Our prayers are mostly for our own psychological benefit and comfort. Others understand God as so immanent in their affairs that they pray that they will find a parking space within a closer walking distance to the Super Target.

Although I don't pray to God for parking spaces—or, I should say that I don't pray that *often* for a close space—I believe that God is immanent. I'm a panentheist. In other words, I believe that God is like a pregnant mother, and we are God's child. We are separate from God, but God surrounds us, and it is in God that we live and move and have our being.

I also like the metaphors of Meister Eckhart. Eckhart was a mystic who said that God is like an artist who works with wood. God has the perfect piece of furniture in mind. We are the furniture, being shaved, sanded, and chiseled into that form. So we exist in the mind of God. We emanate from God's love, and we will return to God's love.

Christian Piatt

We Christians tend to argue about a lot of things, but this is one of our favorites. The short answer is that there is no single understanding of God, nor is there a consensus on how to connect meaningfully with God, to be found in the Christian faith. There was a time when the one, single, unified Catholic Church dictated such theology and rituals, but even then, do we really think that all of Christianity's faithful believed the same thing?

My eyes were opened to the breadth of understanding of God when I started using a God Image Survey in some of the workshops I facilitated. Even people within a single denomination, or even the same church, had incredibly diverse understandings of God. In fact, some people rejected outright the very notion of a "God image."

My own personal understanding of God is always changing, but author and philosopher John Caputo has resonated with me most recently with his explorations of the nature of God. He says that, and I'm paraphrasing, God as some supernatural being doesn't exist. Rather, God is the insistence—the impetus, the inspired breath—that calls all else into existence.

How do we connect with such a God? The way I see it, we simply have to acknowledge the divinity of creation itself, all around us. And that includes us, which means I don't have to look very far.

Matthew Paul Turner

Who is...
Matthew Paul Turner

David Sedaris is my writing hero.

This is a very difficult question to answer, mainly because the authors of the Bible seemed much less interested in the specifics of "God's nature" than many of us are.

That said, within various parts of the Bible, passages do seem to vaguely hint at almost all of the various opinions and ideas that people have purported and argued throughout history.

I tend to believe that most of the categories that we try to contain God within are inadequate. It seems to me that while God is "other," God has chosen to saturate all of creation with God's presence.

While I'm really not one to dodge the question by playing the "it's a mystery" card, I also think that in this case it may be an appropriate card to play.

101

I suspect that whatever answer I come up with or somebody else comes up with, the truth doesn't fit our pre-established categories. God's nature is complicated and confusing and the Bible doesn't really make any effort to make it less complicated and confusing.

God is mysterious, and the Bible embraces the mystery. As much as we want God to be like a frog as we play the role of the eighth-grader with a scalpel, the Bible resists this analogy at every turn. After all, a manageable God that we could clearly understand and classify wouldn't be a God at all, but an idol.

Brian Ammons

A. Yes. Christians believe all of those things, or at least some Christians believe each of them, and most Christians believe some combination of them. I experience God as both transcendent and immanent (right here, right now). Because the Christian tradition holds that God walked among us in the form of Jesus, the immanent presence of God is central. And if we are indeed created in God's image, then some of who God is is revealed in each of us.

In my day-to-day life, I think about God as *Story*. As Story, God is the very process of meaning-making in the world. *Story* (capital S—God, the big Story) contains and functions through *stories* (lower-case s—the stories we tell to ourselves and one another). God, therefore, is not simply *in* the narrative, but is narrative *itself*; exists not simply as the reservoir of all possibilities, but in those very possibilities. It's a bit of an abstract idea, but it's how the transcendent and "right here, right now" play together in my life to make meaning.

Scriptural reference(s):

Genesis 1:27
John 3

Suggested additional sources:

- *The Triune God: An Essay in Postliberal Theology* by W. C. Placher
- *The Weakness of God* by John Caputo
- *What Would Jesus Deconstruct? The Good News of Postmodernism for the Church* by John Caputo
- *Insurrection: To Believe Is Human; to Doubt Divine* by Peter Rollins

Questions for further discussion/thought:

1. How do you imagine God? Where does that image come from?
2. How does it make you feel when you come across other understandings of God that are radically different from yours?
3. What do you think about John Caputo's claim in Christian Piatt's essay above, about God's insistence, rather than God's existence, being of primary importance?
4. What do you believe about the nature of God? Do you believe that God is immanent or transcendent?

Source cited:

- Meister Eckhart, *The Thought of Meister Eckhart* (Mahwah, N.J.: Paulist Press, 1981)

There has been a lot of media attention paid to "end times." What do Christians really believe about the so-called apocalypse described in Revelation?

Christian Piatt

Who is...
Christian Piatt

In college I was the lead singer for several rock bands and had hair down to my waist.

I've always dreaded the well-worn Christian question: "If you died today, do you know where you'd spend eternity?"

For starters, no one *knows* with complete certainty. If we did, we wouldn't have a need for faith. Second, I think we have to reframe the whole notion of "eternity," as if it's some far-off thing that starts only after you die. Eternity, by definition, has no beginning and no end, and, as such, that means we're living in eternity right now!

This question also leans on the tried-and-true evangelism tool of fear to try and coerce people into the faithful fold. Though fear is a powerful motivator in the short term, I don't think it's something upon which to found one's faith, or the reason people should decide what they're going to commit the rest of their lives to.

I watched a documentary recently, called *Hellbound?*, which explores questions around the doctrine and Christian understanding of hell. For me, the question that the director asked (to someone screaming at passersby about the fiery pits of hell) struck a real chord:

"How many kids do you have?" he asked the man.

"Three," the man responded.

"And which do you love more?" he asked. The man had no response. He went on to ask the sidewalk preacher which of his beloved children he would cast out forever for something they did—or didn't do—distancing himself from them forever. The man was, understandably, speechless.

If we, as human beings, have such capacity for love, mercy, and forgiveness, how much greater must the love, mercy, and forgiveness of our Creator be?

104

Phil Shepherd, *a.k.a.* the Whiskey Preacher

I have an epic fear of snakes, an "India Jones" fear of snakes. I hate them with a passion. Fortunately for me, Alaska is one of the few states in the Union that doesn't have a population of snakes, unless you're at a pet store. Not having to deal with snakes growing up was one of the many perks of growing up in the "Last Frontier," and it freed up my anxiety for more pressing issues, such as being prepared for the second coming of Jesus.

As a Southern Baptist, I was taught to believe in a literal second coming and the "end times," horrific events that were believed to lead up to Jesus' return. These events included wars, famine, earthquakes, and other "apocalyptic" catastrophes. It was not the return of Jesus that scared me; it was the waiting part that scared me, having to endure these "signs of the times."

I live in Texas now, and although it has snakes and is somewhat smaller than Alaska, I love it here. I no longer have a faith based in fear, spending sleepless nights worrying that I will be "Left Behind." I now try to live in the present, searching for where Jesus is already active and present in the here and now: a newborn baby's cry, the touch of Stephanie's hand, a slug of fine whiskey, or a puff from a well-crafted cigar. Jesus is already here. Sometimes we simply have look beyond our fears to find him.

Two Friars and a Fool

Who is...
Two Friars and a Fool

One of us is real and the other two are elaborate hand puppets.

A lot of media attention has been paid to "end times," but for the most part none of it has any more to do with Christianity than it does with misinterpretations of the Mayan Calendar or the scribblings of Nostradamus. Throughout Christian history, every few years people have gathered *en masse*, convinced that the end times had come, and they haven't been right yet.

Worse, the elaborate fictions that get billed as biblical prophecies turn the gospel on its head. Instead of the good news of God's coming reign of peace, it becomes a horror show of torture and violence, with a laser-beam-eye Jesus gleefully disintegrating sinners at the center of it all. These violent and xenophobic visions are anti-Christ.

Part of the reason for the curiosity about end times is that the prophets, and then Jesus and Paul and others, were very excited about imminent change in the world. Paul even said not to bother getting married because this great change was coming so soon it wouldn't matter. Modern-day prophets such as Martin Luther King Jr. frequently referred to the "arc of the universe" bending at last toward justice.

This language about impending change for the better was never intended to cause us to check days on our calendars or set our alarms or stare at the sky expectantly. Apocalyptic language is there to remind us of what God is doing in our own lives, and that God will not give up on the world until we are all healed and reconciled.

Scriptural reference(s):

Revelation 6
Revelation 21:1–4

Suggested additional sources:

- *Hellbound?* (Documentary film)
- *Love Wins* by Rob Bell
- *Reading Revelation Responsibly: Uncivil Worship and Witness: Following the Lamb into the New Creation* by Michael Gorman
- *Discipleship on the Edge: An Expository Journey Through the Book of Revelation* by Darrell W. Johnson
- *The Theology of the Book of Revelation* by Richard Bauckham

Questions for further discussion/thought:

1. Do you believe in hell? Who do you believe goes there, and why? Is it forever?
2. How does your understanding of hell inform your daily faith walk? Your understanding of God?
3. What work do you see God doing in the world? What impending change for the better would get you excited about the future?
4. If you were God, what would you do to make things right in the world? Can you think of any reason God wouldn't do the same things you would?

5. Let's say you somehow know the date that the end of history will come. Would you live your life any differently, knowing that time was limited and that the world had an expiration date?
6. Did you come from a faith tradition that believes in the end times? If so, how has that affected your view of the world?
7. Is it possible that there are different views of what the book of Revelation is trying to communicate, and, if so, what do you think they are?

Sources cited:

- *Raiders of The Lost Ark*, Paramount Pictures, 1981
- *Left Behind* by Tim LaHaye and Jerry B. Jenkins (Wheaton, Ill.: Tyndale House Publishers, 1996)

Do Christians still believe that wives should submit to their husbands? What do they mean by "submit"?

Margot Starbuck

Who is...
Margot Starbuck

I met my birth mom when I was 22 years old.

The stereotype of those who favor the submission of wives to husbands, and women to men, can elicit images of creepy Stepford Wives and women in church with duct tape over their mouths. To be fair, though, Christians who maintain women's submission usually have something less evil in mind. These would suggest that men have a God-given authority, and responsibility, as heads of household and leaders over women.

Many others, like me, and also my husband, believe that, in Christ, the former distinctions and hierarchies between Jew and Greek, slave and free, male and female have been erased (Gal. 3:28). As it was in the beginning (Gen. 1:26–27), the image of God is reflected in both male and female.

The temptation for folks like me, though, is to throw the baby out with the bathwater. Specifically, because of the historic ways the word "submit" has been abused, we're tempted to scrap it altogether both in our vocabulary and also in our relationships. The fact is, Paul's teaching on submission has a lot more to say to husbands than it does to wives! Husbands, said Paul, are to love their wives the way Christ loved the church. That Christ died for the church makes me, as a woman, actually suspect I got the better deal! Marriages do thrive when, in humility, love, and service, wives and husbands submit to one another.

Andrew Marin

When I asked my wife about this question, she responded with, "Phhhh. They better not believe that anymore." I guess that's the answer in my marriage.

Theologically, the New Testament uses the word "submit" and its variations seventy-six times, with no one escaping its inclusion, even as far as Jesus' unenthusiastic submission to the will of God for his death.

As for the particular passage in question (Eph. 5:22–23), it's important to note that the literal Greek can be translated, "Wives, to your husbands as to the Lord" (v. 22). The Greek for "to submit" is absent from the original text. This shows that verse 21, then, is a transitional statement of submission, whose broader context includes Christ, wives, husbands, and the Church (vv. 21–33).

If both husbands and wives are to submit to, and love each other as to the Lord, a free-will submission is being described. The Lord does not make any-one submit; it's a choice we all have to make. Therefore, just the same occurs in a marriage relationship, both partners must choose to submit to each other out of love and reverence.

Finally, Paul is writing in a context where men were culturally and reli-giously dominant over women and the family. Though the exact term in verse 23 is translated as "head," that is bound by specific words in time and place. The overarching principle of mutuality in submission by husbands, wives, and Christ throughout the larger passage is what transculturally applies to con-temporary society.

Jonathan Brooks

Who is...
Jonathan Brooks

I could eat pizza every day and never get tired of it.

This verse is found in Ephesians chapter 5 and is meant to be a liberating passage for women who were treated as property. The original Greek word translated here as "submit" is more accurately translated as "attached to or identified with," and Paul was addressing the fact that women, even after being married, could still be identified with their fathers (if brought back home at least twice a year), and thus their endow-ments and property could continue to be held by the father. This is why Paul later quotes Genesis when he says a man should *leave* his father and mother and be joined to his wife (Eph. 5:31, referring to Gen. 2:42). The passage begins with the words "submit yourselves one to another" and is followed by the command for husbands to love their wives as Christ loved the church (Eph. 5:25). The passage is also translated using the word "head" to represent the man's relationship to the woman and Christ's relationship to man. The Greek word originally used there is actually better translated as "source." It actually reads that man is the source of woman and Christ the source of man. Similar to the head of a river being its source, this refers to the Christian view that Eve was taken from the rib of Adam. The verse is about the way Christ loves the church and is not at all about husbands' supremacy over wives. It is a liberating passage that puts more pressure on husbands to treat their wives with great respect and to love them as Christ loves the church.

Scriptural reference(s):

Genesis 1:26–27
Matthew 26:42
Galatians 3:28
Ephesians 5:21–33

Suggested additional sources:

- *Choose Love Not Power* by Tony Campolo
- *Four Views on Free Will* by John Martin Fischer, Robert Kane, Derk Pereboom and Manuel Vargas
- *Hard Saying of the Bible* by Walter C. Kaiser Jr., Peter H. Davids, F.F. Bruce, and Manfred T. Brauch
- *Did St. Paul get Jesus Right?* By David Wenham
- *Christians for Biblical Equality* http://www.cbeinternational.org/
- *Christian Feminism Today*: http://www.eewc.com/
- *Gender and Grace* by Mary Stewart Van Leeuwen

Questions for further discussion/thought:

1. How do you look at your spouse—in mutuality, through the lens of submission, or a combination of both?
2. How does the view of your spouse influence your relationship with the Lord and the Church?
3. In a marital relationship, what would mutual submission look like to you?
4. Which do you think is more difficult: submission or unconditional love?
5. Take a stab at defending the position you do not hold. If you're an egalitarian, can you think of any legit reasons others might hold another position?

Source cited:

- *The Holy Bible*

Is the Christian God the same God as the God of Islam and Judaism? If not, what's the difference? If so, why have three separate religions?

Bart Campolo

Who is...
Bart Campolo

I spend most of my time working for a two-state solution to the Israeli-Palestinian conflict.

I think a better question might be whether the Gods of any two writers in this book are the same, or whether the God of John Piper is the same God as the God of Rob Bell, or, while you're at it, whether Paul's God was the same as Matthew's, or Mark's, or Luke's, or John's. The answer, of course, all depends on your point of view.

From their perspective, all of my friends and relatives would say that they know the same Bart Campolo, and on one level they would all be right. On another level, however, each one of them has a different understanding of who I am, how I think, and what I want.

Part of that is because I have gotten to know each of them in different ways, under different circumstances, and at different levels of intensity. Another part, of course, is that each of them is at a different place in his or her life, with different capacities and different needs, which causes me to share myself with them differently. A final part, I'm afraid, is that some of them are morons who totally misunderstand me no matter how hard I try to set them straight.

There's only one God, I think, and we've all got that God wrong in our own way. Let's just hope Jesus was right about all that grace.

Hugh Hollowell

Who is...
Hugh Hollowell

I pastor people who are often homeless. I used to sell mutual funds. Heck, I used to own mutual funds.

The other two religions seem to think so. The prophet Mohammed was sure he was worshiping the same god the Jews and Christians were (see, for example, Qur'an 29:46), and the apostles thought they were worshiping the same god Moses and Abraham knew. Both Arab Muslims and Arab Christians pray to Allah, which is just the Arabic word for God, and Spanish Muslims, Christians, and Jews all pray to Dios, the Spanish name for God. The English word "god" is probably less than 800 years old.

They all worship the same God. Where they differ is how they think this God is decisively known. Jews think God is known by the covenants God has made, Muslims think God is known through the Koran, and Christians believe God is known through the person of Jesus. One God, three religions.

Two Friars and a Fool

Who is...
Two Friars and a Fool

One of us was not baptized until he had already gone through a couple years of seminary.

From God's point of view, yes. If we trust that there is a real God who exists outside our imagination, then that God is really out there somewhere, and human longing is aimed at that God one way or another. There is not a God competition where the weakest God is voted off the island. There's just God, and our incomplete attempts to understand.

From the point of view of the various faiths that profess belief in a God, though, we have to say no. Christianity, Judaism, and Islam ask different questions and come to different answers. It is a little bit disrespectful, if you think about it, to say that "we all believe in the same God," or that these three faiths can be described with the bland term "Abrahamic." There's a lot more than Abraham going on in Christianity, Judaism, and Islam, including significant disagreements both on details and on big themes.

These differences freak some people out in each of the three traditions, but we wouldn't expect it to be any other way. We have an infinite, transcendent God, who literally embodies mystery, breaking into our human experience in various ways. These differing experiences of God will lead to differences in understanding, language, and practices. Christian scripture is an ongoing argument between voices that disagree on significant questions. This just mirrors our experience in the world. Out of all this dealing with real differences, we come to understand more about God and ourselves, not less.

Suggested additional sources:

- http://www.patheos.com/Library/Islam.html
- http://www.patheos.com/Library/Judaaism.html
- http://www.huffingtonpost.com/charles-kimball/whither-the-clash-of-civi_b_823631.html
- *Allah: A Christian Response* by Miroslav Volf
- *The World Religions* by Huston Smith

Questions for further discussion/thought:

1. What beliefs or practices of another religion are you curious about? What beliefs or practices do you engage in that someone of another religion may be curious about?
2. In many Western societies right now, we are hearing more and more about a "clash of civilizations," often with one side identified as Christian or "Judeo-Christian" and, on the other side, Islam. What possibilities exist between this so-called "clash of civilizations" on the one hand and the idea that "all Abrahamic religions are basically the same" on the other?

Why do so many churches not allow women to serve in positions of leadership? Have they not read the scripture in Galatians 3:28 stating that "there is neither male nor female"?

Jonathan Brooks

Who is...
Jonathan Brooks

I once jumped from the roof of a two-story building (crazy graffiti artists!).

A. Many churches do not allow women to serve in positions of leadership because of a misunderstanding of the apostle Paul's teaching on gender roles in the church. I have to honestly say there was a time when I didn't understand this passage and could not reconcile Jesus' position on women with Paul's. I have since come to realize that Christ and his teachings and actions endorse the full inclusion of women in leadership roles. Paul's words on women are actually an endorsement for their inclusion in worship and their gaining of knowledge.

In the Corinthian church, women were used to being separate from their husbands in worship (as was the Roman tradition), and thus had to trust them for understanding. Paul is dismissing this idea and telling women they are to seek knowledge for themselves and that they should seek information from their husbands who had been properly educated. This in turn meant men should be willing to share this knowledge. This is not an indictment on women but an encouragement, and it is not a biblical endorsement for the supremacy of men but a command to equal the playing field. Of course, some people will always see the glass as half empty rather than half full.

Margot Starbuck

Although I'm, *technically*, a church leader with a vagina, I am so grateful to have *not* experienced the kind of resistance that many women leaders have experienced. Having seen a female associate pastor in the church where I was raised (this is big!), and always being encouraged by my family to be whatever I set my mind to be, it simply never occurred to me that I ought not be a bearer of God's word. But though I wish it were otherwise, folks who are opposed to women in leadership are not going to roll over just because Galatians says that dividing lines have, in Christ, been erased.

Churches who hold this position believe that men were created by God to be in authority over women. The scriptural justification for this is, in my opinion, a little shaky. In his first letter to the Corinthians, Paul teaches that women should be silent in churches. I might have said the same thing to folks who did not have access to equal education as men! The position that women across all times and places ought not speak in churches simply does not align with the larger biblical witness, nor the witness and practice of Jesus. Peek at Scott McKnight's little e-book *Junia Was Not Alone* for more on women in the New Testament church.

Sean Gladding

My guess is those churches *have* read Galatians 3:28. But they have also read more of Paul's letters, and based on passages such as 1 Timothy 2:12, 1 Corinthians 14:34–35, and 1 Timothy 3:1–7, they have concluded that women were and are ineligible for the leadership of God's people. Two hundred years ago, some churches read Galatians 3:28 ("there is neither slave nor free") while endorsing slavery as a biblically sanctioned institution, yet I cannot think of one church today that would claim that the Bible supports that evil practice. Clearly we can change our minds on what the Bible does and does not sanction.

So why do some churches not allow women to serve in leadership? In my most generous moments, I think they do so out of sincere belief in their interpretation of scripture, and even though they might wish it otherwise, they are "stuck" with this restriction on leadership. However, my experience suggests that such churches are not open to a different reading of scripture on this question because, well, it benefits the men who are doing the interpretation, maintaining their position of power.

The question for such churches is this: if women cannot serve in the leadership of God's people, why do they do so throughout scripture?

- Deborah – the only judge who held that office when she delivered God's people;
- Huldah – the prophet who led the only revival under Israel's kings;
- Priscilla – who corrected Apollos's understanding of the gospel;
- Chloe, Mary, Lydia, Nympha – church leaders all;
- Junia – the apostle.
- If Paul does not permit women to lead, why does he greet women who do?

Scriptural reference(s):

Judges 4:4–5
2 Kings 22:14–20
Acts 12:12
Acts 16:14–15, 40
Acts 18:24–26
Romans 16:1–2, 7
1 Corinthians 1:11
1 Corinthians 14:33–35
Galatians 3:28
Philippians 4:2–3
Colossians 4:15
1 Timothy 2:11–12

Suggested additional sources:

- *What Paul Really Said about Women* by John Temple Bristow
- *Why Not Women* by Loren Cunningham
- *Did Paul Get Jesus Right?* by David Wendham
- *Junia was Not Alone* by Scott McKnight
- *Christians for Biblical Equality* http://www.cbeinternational.org/
- Christians for Biblical Equality's bookstore: http://equalitydepot.com/
- *Christian Feminism Today*: http://www.eewc.com/
- *Women, Ministry & the Gospel* by Mark Husbands and Timothy Larsen
- http://www.ntwrightpage.com/Wright_Women_Service_Church.htm
- *A Woman's Place* by Carolyn Osiek, et al.
- http://rachelheldevans.com/brothers-speak-out-john-piper-masculine

Questions for further discussion/thought:

1. How has the feminist movement affected this argument?
2. Could you be a part of a church that did not allow women in leadership? Why or why not?
3. What are the benefits, for the Church, of holding the position that women should not be in Church leadership?
4. What are the benefits, for the Church, of holding the position that women should be in Church leadership?
5. How would you answer original question, and why?
6. What consequences have you seen or experienced when only men are in leadership?
7. What has your experience been of women in leadership in the church?

Source cited:

- *The Holy Bible*

Some Christians consider tithing—giving a tithe, or a tenth, of their income—as an obligation. Others have different views about giving. Why the difference of opinion? And does it matter?

Matthew Paul Turner

Who is...
Matthew Paul Turner

As a child, I raised chickens and sold their eggs to make money for college.

Giving tithe and offering is mentioned throughout Scripture. Throughout the Old Testament, we read stories about the Israelites celebrating harvest by bringing a tenth of what they had earned or grown or raised to be set aside for the poor. Tithing wasn't meant to be a grievance; it was a time of celebration and thanksgiving for all that God had blessed them with that year. And what they tithed was brought to together as charity for the poor.

Jesus talked a lot about giving. Sometimes his words about money came in the form of stories or parables, and other times his teachings about finances seemed a little more "off the cuff." But in either instance, when Jesus talked about giving, he didn't focus on the amount or percentages; he seemed far more interested in the giver's heart.

For instance, when Jesus was at the temple and witnessed a poor woman dropping two small coins in the temple's treasury, he made a point to tell his disciples that the woman had given much because she'd given all that she had. For Jesus, it wasn't about the small amount that the woman gave. Jesus pointed this woman out because she had given despite her lack of wealth.

Is tithing an obligation? I think that's a personal decision that each of us must come to on our own. However, I do believe, that if our hearts are focused on Jesus, giving will become a natural part of our spirituality, whether we are rich or poor.

Phil Jackson

Who is...
Phil Jackson

I love going to the movies.

Tithing is our response to God, acknowledging that the strength to work and support our families or ourselves comes from and is sustained by him. We also give to affirm that God is in control of our lives because he loves us, and our love for him should be reflected in our actions as we give. When we give, we are literally saying: *God, this money is your money. You gave me the strength to work and gain it, and it has no control over me or my life. You are the only one who controls my life, and I trust you!*

How much you give should be determined by how much you truly see God in control of your life. The Old Testament stated that people gave at least 10 percent as a rule, but in the New Testament Christ taught that our giving should be sacrificial and from the heart. People must look at what they have to give from, the money they have to spend, and commit it to God. (You can't give what you don't have in hand, before taxes.) Some say no less than 10 percent, because the word *tithe* means a one-tenth part of something, and that this should be the standard and then to go from there. Each situation is different, but the two common aspects that we all can do are, first, to give with love and joy in our hearts for all that God has done and is doing in our lives, and, second, to give sacrificially.

Jesus saw a woman who was a widow who gave two pennies as her offering, but he knew that this was all she had. She gave sacrificially. You and I both know we can go without another pop (or soda) today. We could hand wash the car rather than get lazy and go to the car wash, or we could take public transportation. We could do so much more with less, but because we have let our money control us more than God, we will spend it to stay comfortable rather than to sacrificially go without and give to God's kingdom work. If people gave like they spend on stupid stuff, folks in our hoods would perhaps not go as hungry as they do.

Doug Pagitt

A. Tithing matters to some people and not to others. This difference is a reality on every topic. So, yes, tithing is a really big deal to some. But to me it is not.

Tithing is an ancient practice by which those living in early Mesopotamian culture, as part of the nations of Israel and Judah, paid for their civic, governmental life and paid for their religious system. It was synonymous to giving to the temple as a means of caring for the poor, and making a religious sacrificial gift.

In the world we live in, we divide our civic life and religious systems into separate spheres, so there would be nothing like a tithing system to participate in. Giving to a local church or denominational organization is simply nothing akin to the tithing structure.

We care for the needy in much more complex systems and through many channels in our world—including the government, charities, and our own homes.

Scriptural reference(s):

Leviticus 27:30–32
Luke 21:1–4
Acts 20:35
2 Corinthians 9:7

Questions for further discussion/thought:

1. Why don't people give a tithe?
2. What have churches done to hinder people from giving?
3. What happens when the people of God don't give?
4. What is "giving abuse"?

Question

Why are many Christian holidays, such as Christmas and Easter, so closely related to pagan holidays? Are Christians actually pagans?

Doug Pagitt

Christianity has always existed within and partnered with culture. There is no time when there was a nonculturally specific Christianity. It always takes place within a people who have a language, eat certain foods, and celebrate in certain ways.

In the early days of Christianity, its adherents wanted their faith to make sense to and be an active part of the culture. So, when they wanted to tell the story of the birth of the Promised One who they declared as the "Light of the world," it made sense to put that celebration at the time closest to the Winter Solstice when the days would start getting brighter. So, the Christ Mass was celebrated during the same time as the other religions were telling their story of light coming to the earth.

So, yes, Christianity has its roots in pagan calendar and storytelling, as they were already in practice when the story of Christmas was introduced.

It might come as a surprise to some to realize that Jesus was not born in December, and the 25th is not a birthday party but was the best time to tell that part of the story.

It is yet another reminder that Christianity is not a static, culturally removed belief system but rather the dynamic interplay of the story of God and the lives of real people.

Two Friars and a Fool

Once upon a time, three seminary students went out into the snow-dusted forest behind their rented cabin, seeking to cut down a Christmas tree with a pair of shears. It went about as well as you'd expect. Why would they do this in the first place? There is nothing in the Jesus story about evergreens or tinsel or Uncle Andy getting drunk on eggnog—certainly nothing about spending $450 billion a year on exchanging presents.

Good Christianity is spiced with some paganism. Christian holidays are kind of a remix of Roman and later northern European holidays. Easter, or Estre, is an old pagan goddess who used to accept offerings of painted eggs, and folktales connect her with hares. Pagans burned Yule logs all night during the longest night of the year to symbolize the rebirth of the Sun Child and the return of light and fertility to the land.

The word *pagan* comes from the Latin *"paganus,"* which basically means "rural." Christians have always incorporated the cultures they encounter, adapting some of what they find to help illustrate their core stories. This happened in the Roman Empire when setting dates for things such as Christmas, and in northern Europe when coming up with some of the symbolism of Christian holidays. In America, we've inherited these practices and symbols. In other parts of the world, Christianity looks quite different, and is a combination of what is brought to a new culture and what was already there.

Questions for further discussion/thought:

1. Jesus embraced some traditions of his culture and rejected others. Some of our culture's traditions seem compatible with Christian practice and others don't. How do we discern the difference?
2. Christmas and Easter are, to many people, the two most important Christian holy days. Why are they so different? Why does Christmas include Black Friday and an annual frenzy of purchasing? Why does Easter entail little more than perhaps a sunrise service and an Easter egg hunt? Does one feel more or less holy as a result of all of the differences?
3. How would you feel if Christianity incorporated other cultural holidays, such as Super Bowl Sunday or Independence Day? Or do Christians in your community already do this?

Question

What does "ordained" mean with respect to ministry? How does someone get ordained, or get the power to ordain someone else? What, if anything, does it have to do with a perceived call from God? Some churches ordain within the church themselves and other have committees and such. Why are they different?

Brian Ammons

Who is...
Brian Ammons

I can hold my hands behind my back and pull them over my head without letting go.

I've really struggled with theologies of ordination. Because I tend to be a bit distrusting of hierarchies, and the idea that all Christians are ministers is really important to me, the whole business has been fraught with tension. I was raised in a tradition in which bishops did the ordaining, clinging to a notion of apostolic succession that suggests that those who had been ordained had been ordained by those who had been ordained by those who had been ordained, all the way back to Peter—who was ordained by Jesus to take leadership of the movement. The claim to authority within the church leadership was built on these credentials, an evocation of centuries of tradition connected back to Jesus himself. It's a powerful image, and I still respect it. The problem for me was that I was denied access to it. As a same-gender-loving man, that ordination process looked a lot like those in power standing guard and deeming me unworthy to be considered, despite the fact that they'd baptized me as a infant and claimed me for the church. Fine, then. Keep your ordination. I'll live out my call with or without your permission. That's pretty much how I said it to a room full of ordained clergy in my Divinity School interview.

I changed my mind. A few years later, as I became more grounded in the Baptist tradition I claimed as an adult, I came to understand ordination as a blessing of particular gifts for the service of the church, and a profession of commitment to living out of those gifts. Within a context in which I was ordained by my local congregation, it seemed to make more sense. A community of folks who knew me well stood with me through my discernment to pursue formal theological education, supported me in that journey, and then called me back to minister with their youth and young adults. These folks were naming what they saw in me; they were joining with me in the celebration of particular gifts that the church needs to fulfill its larger purpose. So, I stood before that congregation and looked each of them in the eye as they came forward and laid hands on me in an act of blessing. Though I no longer serve that congregation, I carry that ordination with me out into the world. It's a covenant I made with both God and a community that took a leap of faith with me. I take that very seriously.

Margot Starbuck

Who is...
Margot Starbuck

I enjoy crime shows, real and imagined.

To ordain someone is to set that person apart for a particular type of ministry. In many churches deacons are ordained to serve and meet the needs of the community, and elders are ordained for teaching and leadership. Some churches call a particular type of elder, one who preaches and teaches and administers sacraments—a...wait for it... *Minister of Word and Sacrament*. This person is set apart for a particular type of pastoral ministry.

While some folks—as Joey, on the TV show *Friends*, in preparation to officiate Chandler and Monica's wedding, did—get ordained online or off of matchbook covers, more often a larger church body decides who should and should not be set apart for ministry. It is the body that confirms an person's personal sense of God's calling in that individual's life. If the body decides a person is not "fit" for ministry, their judgment overrules a person's private sense of call.

From the College of Cardinals that elects a Pope, to a Presbyterian nominating committee that selects candidates for elder and deacon, to the pastor of an independent church who leads in identifying other church leaders, the way in which a church ordains people usually matches the style of government the church already employs.

My husband, also ordained, never let his family members call him "the minister" because, *technically*, all Christians are ministers. One who is ordained is simply set apart for a particular type of ministry.

Sean Gladding

My thinking about ordination is rooted in the Story that Scripture narrates, that of God's plan to save the world through a people. The God of the exodus forms that people at Mount Sinai, calling them "a kingdom of priests, a holy nation." Fast forward to the first century C.E., and Peter quotes these words to the Gentiles (non-Jews) who had become part of God's people, the Church. While some were "ordained" in the sense of being set apart for specific roles within God's people, my understanding of the Story leads me to believe that our baptism is our ordination. We are a kingdom *of* priests, not a kingdom *with* priests.

Thus I do not believe in the ontological ordination that some forms of organized church practice, this idea that there is a special class of person who is "set apart" for sacramental service—e.g., able to consecrate the elements of the Eucharist. I do believe in functional ordination, that local communities of God's people may "set apart" members for specific tasks that they are recognizably gifted to do—e.g., preaching, creating and leading liturgy, organizing care for the less resourced; however, this does not make them of a different "class" than the rest of the community of God's people. We are all priests: those called and baptized in order to serve the world that God loves.

Scriptural reference(s):

Genesis 12:1–3
Exodus 19:3–6
1 Timothy 3:1–7
1 Timothy 3:8–13, Acts 6:3
1 Peter 2:9–10

Suggested additional sources:

- Google search: Your denomination name (Methodist, PCUSA, Southern Baptist, etc.) plus "ordination"
- *Missional Church* by Darrell Guder, ed.
- *Liquid Church* by Pete Ward

- *An Emergent Theology For Emerging Churches* by Ray S. Anderson
- *The Forgotten Ways* by Alan Hirsch

Questions for further discussion/thought:

1. As a culture, do we need ordained clergy? What role do they serve in our larger communities?
2. Why do you think it's important to set some folks apart for particular forms of ministry? What type of training would it be important for these to receive?
3. What images come to mind when you hear the word priest?
4. If the priesthood of all believers is not just a nice idea but the DNA of the church, how might that change the way you view yourself?
5. In what ways are you being a priest in the world?

What do Christians believe happens after they die, and why? Do they believe they are judged immediately and are ferried off to heaven or hell? What about purgatory?

Phil Snider

According to the churches I grew up in, those who accept Jesus as their Lord during their lifetime go to heaven. Those who don't go to hell. It's pretty cut and dry. Once this eternal destination is determined, it's irrevocable.

Christians from more liberal traditions aren't quite as certain. Some view heaven as the place where they will reconnect with loved ones, while others see it as a metaphor for the renewal of creation in which God's justice and peace is fully realized.

Few liberals believe in a literal hell where souls are tormented forever. For them, this makes God out to be a cosmic torturer that has much more in common with ruthless tyrants than with Jesus Christ. While this can lead fundamentalists to criticize liberals for not taking God's judgment into proper consideration, liberals agree that actions do have consequences. Not taking care of the environment, for instance, will one day make the earth uninhabitable for human beings. Telling people they will go to hell if they are gay can lead to lifetimes of depression and loneliness. Beginning a war casually can lead to the annihilation of untold thousands of people.

Most Christians agree that actions have consequences. But when the point of Christianity is reduced to going to heaven when we die, the consequences of our actions in this world, of living and loving, of caring and giving, are actually diminished. When Christianity is watered down only to securing one's place in the afterlife, this can lead to, as Peter Rollins notes, "nothing less than a form of nihilism, for the belief in the eternal life [robs] this life of its fragile, fleeting beauty." This isn't to deny the afterlife, but to say that many Christians, including myself, are more interested in life *before* death than life after death.

Matthew Paul Turner

Christians believe all kinds of things about what happens after we die. While I find some ideas to be more compelling than others, all of us are essentially guessing. In the New Testament we do get vague references to resurrection (in contrast to a purely spiritual afterlife), and an insistence that God is "restoring all things" and "making all things new." However, what happens to people who die in the interim is a question that the Bible only addresses indirectly with a handful of dissonant hints. Some parts of scripture imply a sort of awareness, while others seem to indicate something like sleep. Jesus offers a weird parable about a rich jerk and a poor guy named Lazarus, from which some have constructed detailed explanations of what happens after we die. Unfortunately, parables don't tend to work like that, and although the ending seems to be heavily modified by Jesus, the plot appears to be a popular parable in circulation at the time, which isn't original to Jesus.

Some speculate that "time" is a part of the created order and, therefore, God and God's "realm" exist outside of time. In their view, this renders the question somewhat moot, since it removes any interim time period between now and God's ultimate future for those who have died. I like that. Some argue that our loved ones who have died are conscious in the presence of God and are watching over us in some sense. I like that, too. Some argue that the consciousness of those who have died is resting until God fulfills his promises about reconciliation and the restoration of all things. There are days when I find that scenario very appealing as well. The truth is that when it comes to the specifics of what happens after we die, we're basically guessing and hoping. We're in good company, though, because people have been doing this since the beginning of time. However, I am convinced of this: God, who is most clearly seen in Jesus, is love, and God promises that death doesn't have the last word. Love does. I can live with that.

Bart Campolo

Who is...
Bart Campolo

I've been married for 25 years.

Christians believe all kinds of things about the afterlife, but almost all of them believe there is one. I used to think it was a package deal: if you believed in God, then you must believe in the immortality of your own soul, too. And so I did, or at least so I told myself. While heaven and hell had nothing to do with my reasons for becoming a Christian, it literally went without saying that accepting Jesus as my personal Savior meant accepting that such eternal destinations actually existed. It never occurred to me that someone might put their faith in the living God without believing something awaits us beyond the day we die. It only occurs to me now, I think, because I am well on my way to being that someone.

I am no neuroscientist, but I have studied enough to know that each of the many and various parts of my personality has a physical location in my brain, and that if and when that location is altered in some way, my personality will be altered as well. Stimulate my limbic system one way, and I will become more sexually aggressive. Stimulate it a different way and I will become depressed. Damage part of my amygdala and I will become unable to form loving relationships. Damage part of my prefrontal cortex, on the other hand, and I will lose all sense of right and wrong.

In other words, my brain and my soul are essentially one and the same thing. My individual identity is a particular arrangement of particular organic matter over a particular period of time, and when that period comes to an end, that matter will be rearranged into something (or perhaps someone) else. So then, when my ashes return to ashes, and my dust to dust, I reckon Bart Campolo will be no more.

And yet, just as I still believe in a living God, I still believe in eternal life and daily strive toward that goal. I very intentionally love and teach as many children and young adults as I can, trusting that by so doing I become a small part of each one, even as my parents and best teachers became part of me. In this way, I hope to live on through their lives even after I die, and then in the lives of the younger ones they teach and love. As long as that line goes on, I believe, so will I. Even so, my personal immortality is not the point.

The point is that, as one who has so deeply appreciated my own human experience, I am desperate to ensure endless generations have that experience as well. I cannot breathe forever, but this air is so sweet that I want someone to breathe it always. I want someone, many someones, to taste this wonderful food, and to savor this fabulous wine. Having family and friends has been such a joy to me, laughing and dancing and making love have been so delightful, working to exhaustion and then resting has been so satisfying, and raising children so terrifying, believing in God so inspiring, and aging so interesting, that I can't stand the thought that people might cease to do those things. I love life, after all, not just my own life.

Striving toward eternal life, for me at least, is not so much about getting God to punch my ticket for heaven as it is about doing all I can to ensure that humanity itself endures, and in particular that best part of humanity, which scripture calls the "Image of God." It is about asking Grace to guide my thoughts and actions, to literally flow through me into the lives of those who are growing up behind me. It is about keeping the faith by loving my neighbor, and trusting that both of us are thereby becoming part of God's endless love.

Doug Pagitt

Christians have held wildly different views of judgment and afterlife narratives. It is my view that we should understand all the Bible's description of afterlife not as a step-by-step process of what someone will experience as some sort of "five steps to getting your driver's license at the DMV and what to expect when you arrive" listing. Rather, we are to see this language as poetic description of how God brings about righteousness in the world. It is a genre of colorful, big themes of God's work in all creation. Too often people go into the text as if with a scalpel and pull out certain phrases and notions to use literally. God will recreate all of heaven and earth in a much bigger and more beautiful sense than our explanations can ever provide.

Strangely, for all the things the Bible says and all that Christian tradition teaches on so many matters, there is no account from someone who has died to tell us what happens with life. We have no authority on which to speak on these topics. We simply don't know, and have never known. And this limited information has served as "good enough" for billions of people. There is no need to try and overly specify what we can only guess about. Everyone is piecing afterlife explanations together, and this should compel us to hold our views very loosely.

Scriptural reference(s):

1 Corinthians 15:22
1 Timothy 4:10

Suggested additional sources:

- *Love Wins* by Rob Bell
- *What Does the Bible Really Say about Hell?* by Randolph Klassen
- *Surprised by Hope* by N.T. Wright

Questions for further discussion/thought:

1. Do you think Christianity should place more emphasis on heaven or on earth?
2. Do you think Jesus understood his death and resurrection as a necessary transaction so that we could go to heaven?

Source cited:

- *The Fidelity of Betrayal* by Peter Rollins (Brewster, Mass.: Paraclete Press, 2008)

To be a Christian, is it necessary to believe that Jesus really (as in factually) healed the blind, made the lame to walk, rose from the dead, and ascended into somewhere called heaven, where he sits with someone he calls his Father? And if not, why do Christians recite a creed that says that?

Adam J. Copeland

Who is...
Adam J. Copeland

I once ate a meal of potatoes cooked five different ways.

A. Years ago a good friend of mine went through some of the most horrible personal tragedies you can imagine. Through it all, he kept attending church regularly, choosing to sit alone in the balcony. At one point I asked my friend how he was doing with his faith. I wondered how all his struggles had affected him.

My friend told me that there were many Sundays when he woke up and going to church was the last thing he wanted to do. He was angry at God, wrestling with deep questions and wavering belief. But, most Sundays, he did eventually make it to worship.

"On those Sundays," he said, "the most meaningful part of the service is always the Creed. When I am struggling so much with my faith, it's essential for me to hear the faith of the church. When I can't say the words, the church believes for me."

Belief is a funny thing. When my friend stood to hear the Creed recited, part of him knew it was true, or *needed* it to be true, even as he struggled to say the words himself.

As he questioned in his deep grief, did my friend ever cease to be a Christian? I think that's the wrong direction of consideration. Instead, I wonder, *How can the faith of the church support and sustain us in our questions and longing for answers? What power do the stories of Jesus' miracles, death, and Resurrection have for those who long to believe?*

Hugh Hollowell

Who is...
Hugh Hollowell

*My spare time is spent building a garden in
my back yard. It's cheaper than therapy.*

A. I don't think so. (I know good people who disagree with me on this, however.) But even if you don't buy all the claims of historic Christianity, you can still recite the creeds. By way of illustration: If you live in the United States, odds are you have recited the pledge of allegiance to the flag. You probably had no problem doing so. Yet, even the most fervent patriot will agree that we are not "one nation under God, indivisible, with liberty and justice for all." Yet, we say the pledge anyway.

Sharing a creed unites Christians, just like the pledge unites Americans. And while there may not be liberty and justice for all, at our core, the hope of that is what drives the idea of being American. And I may not "believe" that Jesus will come again to judge the wicked and reward the faithful, but the dream of that binds me to the historic faith and to the faithful.

So, I think of it as sort of like the pledge: I don't think it is all going to happen, but I sure hope it does. And saying the creeds in worship binds me with others who hope it does, too.

Phil Snider

A. The vast majority of mainstream biblical scholars emphasize that the Bible doesn't have to be taken literally in order to be taken seriously. This doesn't diminish the value of the Bible, but increases it all the more. The Bible is full of figurative language—parables, narratives, allegories, metaphors, and so on—that operate on a variety of different levels. The more we recognize the poetic quality of religious language, including historic creeds, the more we recognize the enduring value of religion.

Religion is true in the same way that a poem or piece of art is true. To borrow the words of John Caputo: "By the 'religious' I do not mean some preternatural event in a Stephen King novel, or even an extraordinary visitation by a supernatural being like an angel. Of course, that is exactly what Luke's story of the Annunciation to Mary was, but that is a function of great religious narratives, in which we find human experience writ large, the defining features of our life magnified in moving and unforgettable stories, in brilliant religious figures."

Q. *Is it necessary to believe that Jesus healed the blind?*

Experiencing the meaning and depth of Charles Dickens' *A Christmas Carol* doesn't require that you believe in ghosts from the past, present, and future. Neil Gaiman, paraphrasing the great Christian writer G. K. Chesterton, said it best: "Fairy Tales are more than true; not because they tell us that dragons exist, but because they tell us that dragons can be defeated."

Scriptural reference(s):

Luke 1:26–27
Hebrews 11:1
1 Corinthians 13:12

Suggested additional sources:

- *A Good Man Is Hard to Find (Short Story)* by Flannery O'Connor
- *The Heart of Christianity* by Marcus Borg
- *On Religion* by John Caputo

Questions for further discussion/thought:

1. Our modern post-enlightenment understanding of miracles is very different from that of other ages. For you, what is more powerful: facts or stories?
2. What matters more: Christian beliefs or Christian actions?
3. If religion is true in the way that a poem or piece of art is true, how does this influence the way you read the Bible? The way you worship? The way you pray?

Source cited:

- *On Religion* by John Caputo (London; New York: Routledge, 2001)

Question

Many Christians believe that Halloween (at least in its present form) is satanic or the devil's birthday. Why? Can Christians celebrate Halloween?

Jonathan Brooks

Who is... Jonathan Brooks

I once rode an ostrich in South Africa, and I would do it again, dang it!

A. Some of today's popular celebrations associated with Halloween have pagan roots stemming from the ancient Celtic festival Samhain. This harvest festival of the Druids ushered in the New Year, beginning on the evening of October 31, with the lighting of bonfires and the offering of sacrifices. The name "Halloween" comes from the All Saints' Day celebration of the early Christian church, set on November 1 for the remembrance of martyrs. All Hallows Eve, the evening before All Saints Day, began the time of remembrance. "All Hallows Eve" was eventually contracted to "Hallow-e'en," which became "Halloween."

Although Halloween has some aspects of it that can be questionable, there's nothing inherently evil about candy, costumes, or trick-or-treating in the neighborhood. In fact, handing out candy to neighborhood children, as long as you're not stingy, can improve your reputation among the kids! Most Christians are not aware of the origin of the holiday, and some do adopt a nonparticipatory stance. Some opt for alternatives such as Harvest Festivals; many others fully participate (like my family) and just monitor their children's costumes and behavior. Christian's can celebrate Halloween. There is nothing biblical that says we should not. Also, as cool as it sounds, we know about as much about the devil's actual birthday (if he has one) as we do about Jesus': very little.

Sean Gladding

Who is...
Sean Gladding

*The best competitive game of football I
ever played was also my last.*

A. Some churches claim that celebrating Halloween by dressing up in costumes and trick-or-treating is to engage in or at least to glorify paganism, and therefore recommend against doing so. Some offer "Christian" alternatives: "trunk or treating" in the church parking lot or "hell houses." I experienced the latter once, and it was like walking into a living Chick (gospel) tract.

Halloween is not satanic, nor is it the devil's birthday, but it does fall on the same day as Samhain, October 31. Samhain was an important festival for the Celts, marking the end of autumn and, they believed, a night when the spiritual and physical worlds were closest. It is still celebrated by many pagans, but as a distinct festival from Halloween.

Halloween is the contraction of All Hallow's E'en, the night before All Hallows Day, or All Saints' Day. This is a day set apart by the church to remember the saints, particularly those who have died in the previous year. At a church I copastored, All Saints' Day was an opportunity to speak out loud the names of those we had lost, and it was always a healing and powerful experience.

Besides providing a major spike in sales for candy manufacturers and costumers, Halloween seems to be just another holiday. If the church put as much energy and creativity into celebrating All Saints' Day as people do into Halloween, I think we would not need to worry too much about trick-or-treating.

Scriptural reference(s):

Romans 2:14–16
Colossians 2:14
Hebrews 10:27
1 Peter 5:8

Suggested additional sources:

- *Halloween: An American Holiday, an American History* by Lesley Bannatyne
- *Death Makes a Holiday: A Cultural History of Halloween* by David J. Skal

Questions for further discussion/thought:

1. What are some personal safeguards you could put in place during the Halloween holiday to keep your family safe?
2. What are some similarities between Halloween and Christmas?
3. What has been your experience of Halloween?
4. Does your community celebrate All Saints' Day? If not, how could you do so?

Sources cited:

- *Grace To You Blog* http://www.gty.org/resources/articles/a123
- http://www.chick.com/seasonal/halloween/

What's the deal with contemporary Christian music?

Hugh Hollowell

The practice of singing together is an ancient one that goes back at least as far as the Gospels, or almost 2,000 years. But even in churches where people sing traditional hymns, it is pretty rare to find songs older than 1800, and there are virtually none we sing anymore that predate the 1500's.

But regardless, all Christian music was contemporary music at one point or another. The apostles did not know the words to *Amazing Grace*, and Martin Luther never sang *Just As I Am*. In fact, for most of history, Christians primarily sang the psalms in worship.

So why did we keep singing these hymns? They were the ones everyone liked. Only time will tell if any of today's songs have the staying power that the worship songs of 300 years ago did.

Jonathan Brooks

Wow, what a loaded question! The better question is what's the deal with contemporary Christians? I will admit I am going to have a slight slant toward a certain type of contemporary Christian music, that is Holy hip-hop and urban gospel music. There are some issues with presentation for some Christians, but overall contemporary music is mostly making God accessible to the common person as well as giving people good music without making them change who God has created them to be. God first got my attention through Christian hip-hop. He finally had my attention enough to really speak to me. There are many differences of opinion about how contemporary music should sound, the views it should express, the issues it should address, and even whether it should be allowed in churches. The bottom line is that, as God redeems people (calls them back to himself), he also desires their gifts and talents for his use. So whether their music is right for you individually really does not matter. The truth is, we need all different kinds of music because God loves and uses all different kinds of people.

Phil Jackson

I don't know! It drives me crazy, too, that there is a disconnect between good music that is culturally relevant and music that will bring it! When music moves from the world to contemporary Christian culture, it seems, at times, to have lost something.

I am a hip-hop head, and, in the Christian hip-hop culture, you have gaps in theology that divide and hurt the rest of the folks who just want good music that is culturally sensitive and biblically accurate. It seems almost as if Christians don't deal with anything and are oblivious to all of life after committing their lives to Jesus. This is what often keeps contemporary Christian music from getting to the root issues of what people deal with and being relevant to their issues.

Music is the number one vehicle that people use to cope and relax, yet some of the contemporary Christian music may stress you out more. There should not be a divide between the pain, joys, and pressures of life that people experience and the hope that Christ is in their midst, and yet a lot of music tends to separate the two as if your issue doesn't matter, so just put it in Jesus. The truth is that it takes a while, sometimes all of our lives, to figure that process out. We need more music that expresses our humanity and how our issues can be found in the humanity of Christ, and then his deity will be recognized later. Artists need to understand that they don't have to put scripture in every song to assure us or God that it is sacred. The message of Christ taught through parables and stories brought life and awakened those who didn't know him to seek him. Artists as well as those who buy their music need to trust that Christ is bigger than their theological view and will work in spite of it.

Scriptural reference(s):

Psalm 24:1
Psalm 150
Ephesians 5:19
Revelation 7:9

Suggested additional sources:

- *The Hip-Hop Church* by Efrem Smith and Phil Jackson
- *Unorthodox* by Tommy Kyllonen
- *The Soul of Hip-Hop* by Daniel White Hodge
- www.crossoverchurch.org
- www.thahouse.org
- www.humblebeast.com

- www.reachrecords.com
- www.crossmovement.com
- www.lampmode.com
- www.sphereofhiphop.com
- www.rapzilla.com
- www.dasouth.com
- www.3hmp3.com

Questions for further discussion/thought:

1. What would the world be like if everyone was the same?
2. Do you believe that God values variety? Why?
3. Does style of music keep you from enjoying the message? If so, should the music change or should you change how you listen?
4. What songs define our faith now in the twenty-first century?
5. What songs outside of our faith are of substance that speak truth to our faith?

Source cited:

- *My Life!* by Jonathan Brooks

Question

Christians talk about doing the will of God and use the Bible as a reason for their actions, but the Bible and tradition list so many things that one could not do all of them at once. Is there an actual Holy Spirit left by Jesus to provide guidance and counsel? If so, how does one "hear" this guidance and what does it take to have access to it? Can one be led by the Holy Spirit without being a Christian?

Andrew Marin

Who is...
Andrew Marin

As a lifelong Chicago Cubs fan, their utter inability to win a World Series has taught me more about faith through perseverance then just about anything else.

I fully believe there is an active Holy Spirit working in people's lives throughout contemporary society. The Bible tells us that the Holy Spirit is an integral part of God's revelation to us in the sense of knowing the Lord more fully through revelations to believers and nonbelievers alike (Rom. 1:19 and 2:29; Col. 1:9; 1 Jn. 5:20; Jn. 10:3; 1 Cor. 1:18–23).

The Bible also says the Holy Spirit continues work in a believer's life through four main categories: (1) teaching believers all things and bringing to their remembrance all that Jesus has taught them (Jn. 14:12); (2) assisting believers in being witnesses for Jesus (Jn. 15:26–27); (3) bringing about conviction in one's life for one's sin (Jn. 16:8); and (4) guiding believers into all of God's truths to glorify Jesus (Jn. 16:13–14).

In an unscientific or theological fashion, I believe that the little voice in the back of our heads that speaks of good, love, and redemption, and urges us to do what is right—what people today call a "conscience"—can also be labeled as the Holy Spirit speaking. The voice of the Holy Spirit is calling us to live a more faithful, God-based life in the here and now. Romans 1:19 says knowledge of God through the Holy Spirit has been given to us all, whether believers or not, and it is on us to listen and activate that faith.

Carol Howard Merritt

Who is...
Carol Howard Merritt

I paint.

A. If there's a person of the Trinity (Creator, Christ, and Spirit) to whom I relate most, it's the Holy Spirit. Perhaps it's because Jesus speaks of the Spirit as undeniably feminine when Jesus told Nicodemus that he had to be born of the Spirit.

The Spirit is like any person in that there is no way to hear the Spirit unless we listen. So we can set aside time each day to breathe and listen. It's often difficult to do, as a working mom. Yet, in the small hours of the morning, I sit on the edge of my bed, trying to hear the steady rhythm of my breath, and then if there is anything else. Other times I walk. I hear the crunching of my footsteps, and then the singing birds draw my attention upward. I realize the world enveloping me, and I listen. I learn from the words of Thich Nhat Hanh, a Buddhist monk, when I'm caught in traffic. He says to imagine the brake lights in front of us as the eyes of the Buddha. We see the lights, and they remind us to smile and breathe.

The Spirit speaks in many ways. Often she is like a firefly in my thoughts. I know something beautiful is flickering, but the light goes out as soon as my attention is focused. Sometimes the Spirit helps me to sort out a problem that has been plaguing me. Other times the Spirit shows me the next step that I need to tread. Many times the Spirit gives me a sense of empathy, and I begin to understand the pain in someone else's life. Often, the act of listening to my breath simply slows my anxiety and gives me perspective.

A danger lurks in all of this. As we listen for the Spirit, we dare not imagine that our thoughts are God's thoughts and our ways are God's ways. We should not delude ourselves into arrogantly imagining that we are God. We can, instead, cling to humility as we hope for wisdom, and understand that any revelation is just a small glimpse of what we are to do or to be.

Most religions have similar practices that help us become more fully human. I believe that God can work through any person.

Christian Piatt

Asking a mainline protestant about the Holy Spirit is a little bit like asking a Prius owner about NASCAR. We don't dwell too much on what exactly the Holy Spirit is, and what role it plays in our daily faith walk.

Maybe this is a mistake.

I have learned more about the Holy Spirit from worshiping and talking with my evangelical brothers and sisters, most of whom claim a passionate connection to the Holy Spirit. I have felt things in Charismatic worship that are exhilarating and unfamiliar, but I believe the Holy Spirit is much more than a passing feeling. I've sensed God in nature, and in the breeze around me (something to which the Holy Spirit is compared to in scripture,) but again, there's got to be more to it than that.

I'm not exactly a Trinitarian (belief in the Holy Trinity of Father, Son, and Holy Spirit); I consider myself more of an "infinitarian," in that I see God expressed in innumerable ways. But the way I've come to understand the Holy Spirit as part of the Trinity is based on how God's expressions connect us together.

God, the Father is "God beyond."

Jesus, the Son, is "God with."

The Holy Spirit is "God among."

As such, it requires community to invoke the Holy Spirit. Whenever two or more are gathered together in a spirit of longing for God, I believe the Holy Spirit responds.

Matthew Paul Turner

The "will of God" is a confusing topic, mostly because we humans struggle with how we are supposed to associate God's will into our everyday lives. On one hand, we understand that God wants our love and devotion and desires that we love other people. Taking care of the poor, according to scripture, also seems to be of great importance to God. Pursuing those things seem to be actions that God desires, regardless of the details of our lives.

Where this topic becomes tricky is when we begin to wonder and speculate about what "God's will" might be in our individual circumstances. *Should I take the job? Am I supposed to marry him/her? Is God calling me to be a missionary in Kenya?*

143

In the Garden of Gethsemane, Jesus said that he would not leave us alone, that God would be sending his spirit to counsel us through life. People vary greatly on the methods they use to pursue interaction with God's spirit. Most of us pray. Some of us meditate. Others seek the involvement of church community to help them navigate where God's spirit is leading. Oprah has said God's spirit feels like a "nudge" or a "gut feeling." I think people should seek "the Counselor" in ways that are comfortable for them, because I believe that God's spirit is all around us and leading us in conscious and subconscious ways. And we don't control God's spirit. It leads who it wants.

Acts describes God's spirit as a mighty rushing wind. And while we are able to study the wind, and know from which direction is blows, and see and feel its effects, we cannot control the wind. The same is true for God's spirit. Sometimes we can feel it and see it affecting our lives. But we can't control it. Nor should we try.

Scriptural reference(s):

Psalm 46
John 3:8

Suggested additional sources:

- *Christian Theology* (second edition) by Millard J. Erickson
- *The Artist's Way* by Julia Cameron

Questions for further discussion/thought:

1. Have you ever felt you were led in a certain direction or thought that was directly from God through the Holy Spirit?
2. Has there been a time in your life when you were sure that you somehow heard the Spirit? What was that experience like?
3. Before you professed a belief in God, did you feel an urging in your spirit or actions toward something greater?
4. Is the Holy Spirit important in your own faith? What role does it play?
5. The "Father" and "Son" expressions of God are clearly masculine. Do you understand the Holy Spirit on more feminine terms? Gender neutral?
6. Do you have a particular practice for listening to God?

Source cited:

- *Peace Is Every Step* by Thich Nhat Hanh (New York: Bantam Books, 1991)

Why is the church growing in Africa and Asia, but declining in Europe and the U.S.?

Adam J. Copeland

Who is...
Adam J. Copeland

I have dual citizenship with the U.S. and U.K. (my mom's from Scotland).

Complicated factors are at work in global church growth and decline, many of which are cultural. For instance, much of the West's scientific rationalist approach to life makes a false dichotomy between science and religion. If the cultural norms say that curious, open-minded people cannot be Christian, then the church will certainly falter. Along those same lines, some people mistakenly believe we have evolved past a time when we need religion, as if technological progress can replace God, sin, and death.

We are also at a time in the West when, for believers and nonbelievers, the church is often less than compelling. When pastors ride around in Bentleys, and many denominations debate human sexuality more than how to end poverty, the church certainly could be cited as the cause of its own decline.

My stream of the Christian tradition emphasizes that it's the work of the Holy Spirit that grows the church rather than primarily efforts of our own. Perhaps the Spirit, then, is particularly primed to work in Africa and Asia, where God's good news might feel more immanent, powerful, and life-changing.

Before you jump to the conclusion that the Spirit has stopped working in Europe and the U.S., however, consider another possibility. Perhaps it's those of us in Europe and the U.S. who have abandoned God, not the other way around.

Phil Jackson

Who is...
Phil Jackson

I love hip-hop culture, not rap, but real mc's.

A. Churches in Europe and the U.S. are dry and lifeless. Let's just be real and call it what it is. There is not a sense of urgency for God that fuels the passion to serve in powerful ways. The church in America is simply tolerated, but not celebrated as a force for God to build His Kingdom.

The churches in Africa, Asia, and elsewhere are often serving from places of suffering. Often there are threats of persecution if they share with others about their faith in Jesus, or even have a church service. If you have ever been in a situation where you were suffering or in place of urgency for your life, you understand the desire of people in these other countries to passionately seek help from anywhere, looking for a miracle. The Church in the U.S. has stopped looking for anything except air conditioning in the summer, heat in the winter, and a funny yet comfortable sermon that makes them feel good.

The church in America has been hijacked from Jesus by politics and prosperity Gospel that have all sought to keep things safe for those who attend their church. This is not what Christ has called us to be; we are to help invoke God's Kingdom here on earth, yet the church in America has overlooked so many issues of injustice, morality, care for the poor, and generally has settled for a Christ without suffering.

Churches in the U.S. have lost our toughness. We have mistakenly come to believe that church is a place to be comfortable, rather than being a place of constant struggle for justice. There's a lot we can learn from our Christian brothers and sisters on other continents.

Scriptural reference(s):

Matthew 25:40
Matthew 22:36-40
Matthew 28:16–20
Acts 2:37–42

Suggested additional sources:

- *The Next Christendom: The Coming of Global Christianity* by Philip Jenkins
- *Living for Jesus without Embarrassing God* by Tony Campolo

Questions for further discussion/thought:

1. If you were God, would you grow the church evenly around the world or not?
2. What are the signs of healthy church growth?
3. What in your community doesn't reflect your understanding of God's Kingdom? What more can you do to be Jesus in that area and to help God's Kingdom come?

Some Christian teachings are easy, such as loving our neighbor. Others, not so much. For example: the Trinity; what happens at the end of time; and salvation (from what? to what?). Can someone be Christian and not clear about very much?

Two Friars and a Fool

Who is...
Two Friars and a Fool

All three of us married up and parent in a way that can only be described as a la carte.

Believing correctly is the least important thing that a Christian is called to do. It actually drives us crazy that Christians are referred to as "believers." If we're supposed to go around believing things, who cares? Beliefs don't matter if they never lead to action, and actions can reinforce and even change beliefs. We are called to trust God, sure, but more importantly, we are called to *do*—to act.

What's scary are the Christians who are sure they understand things perfectly, and who want to force everyone else to agree with them in order to be accepted, and who get all mean and finger-pointy when anyone disagrees or asks a question.

Reading the Gospels, we find a Jesus who calls people to do hard, good, right things. However hard you think the Christian life is, it is way harder than that, but the only people whose beliefs Jesus challenged or criticized were the people who were being self-righteous and judgmental toward others. From what we can tell, Jesus preferred the company of sinners—not even ex-sinners, but real, live naughty people.

Teachings that appear easy often turn out to be hard. Ever tried loving your neighbor the way Jesus describes it? How about giving to all who ask of you? Teachings that seem really hard and complicated can be simplified most of the time. The key is to keep journeying, keep asking, and keep trying to lovingly live out whatever wrong theology you happen to believe in.

Bart Campolo

Who is...
Bart Campolo

It takes me 30 minutes to write a good sentence.

Some of my other answers in this book are too long (or at least they were before the editors got to them), but this one won't be.

A few years ago, while driving a vanload of high schoolers home from summer camp, I made a clearly illegal U-turn in order to avoid a toll I had paid once already (please don't tell the Pennsylvania Turnpike Commission). As we pulled back onto the highway, one of the kids piped up: "Can a Christian break the law like that?" she asked.

I paused for a moment, searching in vain for an arcane biblical defense, until I found something even better: the simple truth.

"Evidently," I replied.

She looked confused, so I explained further: "I am a Christian. I just broke the law like that. So then, yes, a Christian can break the law like that."

What she was really asking, of course, was whether a Christian *should* break the law like that, but that is not the point. The point is that what makes us Christians is not what we do or don't do, or say or don't say, or understand or don't understand. What makes us Christians is whether we trust that the God Jesus describes in his story of the prodigal son will welcome us home, too, no matter what.

Hugh Hollowell

Have you ever been in a long-term relationship? You loved that person, and that person loved you, and you knew, just *knew*, beyond a shadow of a doubt, that you were loved. Now, you have no idea how the latest sociological research plays into what you felt, or and what part the pheromones in your brain played. But you did not care, because you were in love.

It is a lot like that. Christianity is, above all else, the practice of love. And, so, you don't have to understand how the idea of the Trinity works to love your neighbor, and you need not know how the world ends to feel that, at this exact minute, you are loved by God who wants you to love others.

If you decide you want to understand pheromones, there are books that will tell you everything you want to know, but I don't know that they will make you love any more than you already do. Likewise, once you start trying to catalog faith, it sometimes loses something.

Scriptural reference(s):

James 2:14–26

Suggested additional sources:

* *Insurrection* by Peter Rollins

Questions for further discussion/thought:

1. Are there Christian beliefs that you've encountered that were just downright weird? Can you think of any good reason people might believe that?
2. Have you ever had to hide a belief, or lack of belief, from your community? (Are they watching? If they're watching, just blink once for yes, twice for no.)
3. Is there a belief you know of that is just too far beyond the pale for you to deal with? A belief that if someone said they believed it, you'd have to stop hanging out with them?

Is faith healing really a part of the Christian faith today? What about speaking in tongues? Why do some do it and not others?

Andre Marin

Who is...
Andrew Marin

I qualified for food stamps for three years chasing the vision that is now The Marin Foundation.

I'm all about speaking in tongues. It's Christianity's cool-mega-church-pastor/successful-author's dirty little secret: it's never cool to admit you speak in tongues. One can talk about the active work of the Holy Spirit, but God forbid ever confessing you speak in tongues! In fact, this is the first time for me. It's liberating.

I was raised in an Assembly of God church where the active work of the Holy Spirit, including speaking in tongues, was a part of everyday faith. I got "baptized in the Holy Spirit" my freshman year of college, and ever since then, I have had a running conversation with God through the Holy Spirit throughout the majority of every waking day. Most of the time, I'm speaking in tongues. Sometimes I know what I am saying, and other times I don't. But that is not the important part to me. What is important is that I know I am communicating and communing with God in my spirit all day. The closeness and comfort I feel throughout, even in traumatic times of upheaval, gives me reassurance I am loved and protected.

Here is my dirty little secret: speaking in tongues, whether out loud in prayer or in my spirit throughout the day, is what gives me the strength to continue working everyday to establish kingdom in the most contentious of arenas.

I'm also all about faith healing. Call me crazy, but I believe the miraculous power described in the Bible is just as real today.

Christian Piatt

Who is...
Christian Piatt

I met my wife on a blind date.

A. Faith healing definitely is still a very real part of the Christian experience for many Christians, but I think it's important to define what we're talking about. There is, of course, the kind of speaking in tongues and healing that often take place in a more charismatic Christian worship service. I'd argue that this represents a relative minority of Christians, though.

But do most Christians pray for God's intercession and healing? Absolutely. Such healing takes many forms, too. While some may pray for the physical removal of a disease or other malady, others simply call on God for the peace and courage to endure such suffering. Such healing may not conform to our traditional (or even stereotypical) notions of what faith healing is, but it indeed is an act of faith, calling on God for some kind of salvation.

As for speaking in tongues, I think this also is something that can be open to interpretation. There are those who believe it's all about speaking in a foreign language, but I've never seen or experienced that, personally. What I have experienced is a sort of inspiration, the embers of an idea catching fire with the seeking of God's strength and wisdom. There are times when I speak publicly or write that I get finished and can hardly tell you what I just did.

Is that speaking in tongues? Depends on who you ask.

Phil Shepherd, *a.k.a.* The Whiskey Preacher

A. My friend Bec is a "Tongue Talker," someone who speaks in tongues. I've never personally heard Bec speak in tongues; however, I believe her that she does. Speaking in tongues is so foreign to me that I probably would not know the difference between it or Klingon if I ever heard it. Bec is not pretentious about being a "tongue talker." She doesn't brag that she communicates to God in a different way than I do. She has even had moments of protest, questioning God why she has this ability. But she has come to a place where she accepts what's been given to her.

I also have another friend Kevin who once healed a homeless person who was lame. He's spoken of this incident quietly maybe once or twice over the twenty-plus years I've known him. It's not that he's ashamed of what happened; he simply can't logically explain it, and neither can I. Because Kevin has worked in the medical field for many years and didn't come from a faith background that believed in a healing ministry, it was a surprise to both parties, both the healer and the healed, when this happened.

Predatory ministers who've made their fortunes preying on the vulnerable, lying by faking healing and more, have made us cynical about the mysteries that still float around us today. I would be lying to you if I told you I had an answer for this question. I don't. But just because something can't be explained doesn't mean it's not both real and life-giving.

Scriptural reference(s):

Isaiah 11:2–3
Acts 2:4
1 Corinthians 12:28–31; 14:1–5a, 18–19
1 Corinthians 14:2

Suggested additional sources:

- *Tongues of Fire* by David Martin
- www.Facebook.com/rebeccadawncranford

Questions for further discussion/thought:

1. Have you ever talked to someone who speaks in tongues and asked questions about it? How has that shaped that person's faith journey?
2. Do you believe all the gifts of the Spirit are active in contemporary society? Why or why not?
3. Have you ever witnessed faith healing or speaking in tongues? What did you think about it?
4. Are there other scripturally based ways to understand "gifts of the Spirit" without adhering strictly to the Charismatic Christian expressions of them?
5. What role does mystery play in your faith?
6. Do you believe that God can still heal like in the stories that are in the Bible?

Source cited:

- *Star Trek*

Why are there so many symbolic gestures and images throughout some Christian denominations, while others claim such acts are akin to idolatry?

Two Friars and a Fool

Believing that symbols and images are akin to idolatry is called iconoclasm, and it has a long history.

In an ancient act of iconoclasm, King Hezekiah of Judah destroyed the bronze serpent made by Moses when people's veneration of it seemed idolatrous. When Christianity became the Roman Imperial religion under Constantine, mobs destroyed many statues of other gods. Under the Byzantines, the disagreement over whether icons were an acceptable Christian practice resulted in murders and riots until a second council of Nicaea was called to settle the argument. The iconoclasts lost, but iconoclasm popped up again in the Protestant Reformation when statues of the saints were toppled all over Europe, and many churches adopted a spartan white-washed style still common in the United States.

Iconoclasm is based on the true insight that God is beyond any of our symbols, but how can we point to that which is beyond perception except symbolically? The wisdom of the second council of Nicaea is that symbolism enriches our tradition and helps us connect with truth in a way that abstract thought and words alone cannot accomplish.

The use of images is once again becoming the dominant communication system, a trend exemplified by widespread recognition of the brand Nike from only the "swoosh." The question is whether Christians will embrace our rich iconographic heritage and use this cultural shift to help in the creation and expression of meaning, or whether our heightened visual awareness will be wasted on branding and commercialism.

Brian Ammons

One way to think about this would be to consider differences in worship rituals as akin to differences in literary genres. Some folks love the figurative language of poetry, and some love the straightforward delivery of an encyclopedia entry. You can write a poem and an encyclopedia entry about the same topic, but they are going to require really different genres, and sometimes you become rather attached to them. Nearly every time there has been a move to hold particular gestures and images tightly, claiming that they are essential to Christian practice, some other group questions that understanding. Similarly, nearly every time there has been a move to reject particular gestures and images, some other group reasserts their value.

Part of what draws me into the Christian tradition is that history of wrestling with how we relate to and connect with God. We make idols of our traditions and rituals when we move to thinking they can function as short-cuts through the mystery of God. That can happen in any church, regardless of the pictures on the wall (or lack thereof). We can also consider the traditions of gestures and images (or lack thereof) as invitations *into* sacred Mystery. The church is a mansion with many rooms.

Doug Pagitt

Who is...
Doug Pagitt

As a kid my family had no church experience at all.

Christianity is always a culturally bound expression of the story of God in the past, rebirthed inside the story people are currently living. In some people's culture, imagery is distracting them from their clear-mindedness. For others, the imagery helps focus their mindfulness. This allows people to organize their faith with different practices. Traditions have then tended to solidify their practices into customs. Then people who appreciate that approach find great comfort there, while the others gravitate toward other perspectives. Then this group of like-minded people can begin to see this as "the only way" and give even greater meaning to it, in the end believing that their way is the righteous way. What then does that mean for the other way?

One person's clean, comfortable minimalism is another's cold, barren emptiness. These theological beliefs are often dogma that comes from preferences.

I think we need to be careful of noticing when we make that move from preferences to dogma.

Scriptural reference(s):

Exodus 20:1–18
Exodus 32
Deuteronomy 5:4–21
2 Kings 18:1–4

Suggested additional sources:

* http://www.orthodox.net/faq/protobje.htm
* *The Hidden Power of Electronic Culture* by Shane Hipps
* *Flickering Pixels: How Technology Shapes Your Faith* by Shane Hipps
* *Understanding Media: The Extensions of Man* by Marshall McLuhan
* *Symbol and Icon: Dionysius the Areopagite and the Iconoclastic Crisis* by Eugene F. Ivanovic

Questions for further discussion/thought:

1. What images evoke an experience of God for you? Where do you see windows into sacred Mystery?
2. Charges of idolatry focus on physical symbols, but even mental images, ideas, and titles for God like "father" are mere symbols that fail to accurately depict God. Apart from "father," how many images of God can you come up with?
3. What is your favorite symbol, image, name, or title for God? When you pray, what do you imagine and what names do you use for God?
4. If you pray and/or meditate, try praying or meditating in a different way. If you use an image, try to clear your mind. If you use a name or title, try a different one. Does it make a difference?

Why is personal/individual salvation emphasized so much more in modern Christianity than global transformation of the world into the just peace realm of God's commonwealth? How can one person be saved while others continue to suffer?

Adam J. Copeland

One way to get at this question is through that old favorite verse, John 3:16: "For God so loved the world that he gave his only Son, so that everyone who believes in him may not perish but may have eternal life" (NRSV). This verse is often used in an exclusive way to emphasize the need for personal acceptance of Jesus' love.

There's nothing wrong with mentioning God's love for individuals, but the Greek word that is translated "world" has very corporate shades to it. The word *cosmos* means not "church" or "the people" but "the whole of creation." The emphasis is that God loves all that God has created: you and me, the fields and the fawns, and even (especially?) the world that is alienated from God.

Perhaps our personal/individual approach to faith is connected to the American work ethic that emphasizes personal responsibility. We value individual rights and personal freedom, so much so, in fact, that we forget God necessarily calls us to relationship with others, living out our faith in a world that is all God's to begin with.

With a view toward this more corporate nature of the faith, salvation expands far beyond an individual concern. Salvation is not about what happens to individual souls, but a corporate concern regarding God's whole creation—including people, the earth, and even all life.

Matthew Paul Turner

Perspective is everything here. For those of us in contemporary Western Christianity, our thinking about personal salvation is probably due to the fact that we've been so thoroughly converted to consumerism that we approach everything from that understanding. If we're in the market for some spirituality, we look for the best purveyor of religious goods and services for the lowest cost in terms of time, money, etc. As good consumers, we look for a place (that's right, a church that is primarily a "place" rather than a community) that meets our felt-needs and desires. Unfortunately, churches for the most part have embraced their role in this particular understanding, and they tend to market a gospel to the individual consumer accordingly.

Interestingly enough, in both the Old and New Testaments, the word that is most often translated "salvation" literally means "rescue." I've come to believe that the Christian concept of salvation is rooted in the ancient Jewish concept of *Shalom*, which means something akin to "harmony" between God and people, harmony between people and other people, and harmony between people and God's creation. The assumption is that harmony was broken, chaos is wreaking havoc, but God is reconciling creation back into harmony. God is rescuing us from chaos and fragmentation. Salvation by definition cannot be merely a personal experience. It is inherently relational. Moreover, salvation is not a commodity to be possessed. Those who are being reconciled also become agents of reconciliation. Those who have been rescued by God become agents of salvation. It's not that you "have" salvation. It's that salvation has you.

Phil Snider

Who is...
Phil Snider

The best song more people should know about?
"Cathedrals" by Jump Little Children.

Martin Luther King Jr. once said, "Any religion that professes to be concerned with the souls of men and is not concerned with the slums that damn them, the economic conditions that strangle them and the social conditions that cripple them is a dry-as-dust religion," functioning as "an opiate of the people." I couldn't agree more.

I don't understand how a heavenly paradise can be experienced as anything less than hell if one of my loved ones is suffering, unless while in heaven I could somehow find a way not to care about their fate, which basically goes against everything I've ever been taught about Christian ethics.

We frequently use religion as a means of escaping the world, for the same reasons we might be drawn to drugs or alcohol. We don't want to face the trauma and struggle and heartache that often accompany life, so we repress it as much as we can. We have personal problems we want God to fix, whether now or in the afterlife. Yet at its most profound level Christianity isn't about escaping the trauma that marks our lives by isolating into individualized shells, but rather is about entering into the dark night of the soul together, facing it head on, with the same honesty that Christ displayed on the cross when crying out, "My God, my God, why have you forsaken me?"

It is when we let go of God as the means of escaping the world that we find God.

Sean Gladding

One answer to the question is that we have been shaped far more by our culture than by the Story of God that we have received in scripture. There is little question that the U.S. is a radically individualistic and increasingly narcissistic culture. Growing up, my favorite chocolate bar was Twix: "made for sharing." But by the late '90s the advertising was, "Two for me, none for you." We have done the same with John 3:16. "For God so loved the world…," the world (*"cosmos"*) referring to all that God has created. Now we read it as meaning the collection of individuals who are going to heaven while the world burns.

But is it fair to lay the blame entirely at the feet of culture? Perhaps not. If I think the problem of sin is that I am going to hell, rather than its effect on the entirety of creation, then once I am "saved," all I really need to do is wait to die and tell others that they too can go to heaven. It allows resourced suburban churches to bus poor kids out of my neighborhood for "church" on Sundays, and then drop them off afterward rather than entering the world of their poverty.

I wonder if we do not want the transforming Story of God's kingdom coming, because that would mean having to "work out [our] salvation with fear and trembling" (Phil. 2:12b, NIV). It's much easier to invite Jesus into my heart, and wait to go to heaven.

Scriptural reference(s):

Psalm 139:8
Matthew 27:46
John 3:16
Romans 8:19–22
Romans 12:15
Philippians 2:1–13

How can one person be saved while others continue to suffer?

Suggested additional sources:

- *Hope in the Lord Jesus Christ*, a PC(USA) study paper available for download http://www.pcusa.org/resource/hope-lord-jesus-christ/
- *Stride Toward Freedom* by Martin Luther King Jr.
- *Insurrection: To Believe Is Human; to Doubt Divine* by Peter Rollins
- *The Hole in Our Gospel* by Richard Stearns
- *Velvet Elvis* by Rob Bell
- *The Last Word and the Word after That* by Brian McLaren
- *Salvation Means Creation Healed* by Howard Snyder

Questions for further discussion/thought:

1. Is Christianity as individualistic in other societies?
2. How would you describe salvation?
3. Most of us have felt abandoned by God at some point along the way. Have you ever thought about this as a point of identification with Christ, instead of being contrary to Christ?
4. What is your understanding of "salvation"?
5. Has it changed over the years, and, if so, why and how?
6. How does that shape the way you live your day-to-day life?

Sources cited:

- *The Holy Bible*
- *Stride Toward Freedom* by Martin Luther King Jr. (New York, Harper, 1958), p. 23
- www.Facebook.com/Twix.us

Why do so many evangelicals seem to feel the term "social justice" is a bad thing? Why is it generally associated with leftist political activism?

Andrew Marin

Who is...
Andrew Marin

I am totally obsessed with Giordanos Pizza, Chicago's best, and much better than anything New York produces

Since the invention of language there have been random terms hijacked from one group, opposing another, for political or theological reasons. No word or phrase has inherent value. The values placed on words are socially constructed to serve a purpose. In most cases that purpose has to do with either power or fear mongering—which is still rooted in an attempt to gain power. To vilify a word, phrase, people group, or belief system is the easiest way to rally people around a cause. That is as true today as it was in the Bible.

In regards to "social justice," the rise of the evangelical prostitution of political conservatism caused "social justice" to become an easy target to push a Republican "Christian" agenda catering to the wealthy capitalist more than the poor who are systemically abused by those wealthy capitalists. Theologically, Jesus talks more about justice and protection for the poor than any other topic, which aligns very closely with a social justice ideology.

Yet the convergence of politics, religion, and power has intermarried itself into a nasty incestuous muck, currently unable to reclaim any distinguishable markings that differentiate one term from the next. It is going to take a new set of terms, ones backed up by actions of reconciliatory agents focused on culturally, socially, theologically, and politically pursuing that which is disconnected, to even begin instilling a change of consciousness toward a new understanding of political and religious engagement toward the other.

Phil Shepherd, *a.k.a.* The Whiskey Preacher

Who is...
Phil Shepherd

Feet gross me out.

One part of flying I hate the most is short layovers. Your plane arrives late, there's no time to use a real bathroom that's not the size of a dollhouse, you're rushing to the next gate that's always on the opposite side of the terminal (it's never a pretty sight to watch a stout man run in cowboy boots in the middle of an airport), and you certainly don't get the chance to people watch, which is one of my favorite things to do when traveling. Short layovers are the worst. I try to avoid them as much as possible.

As a former evangelical myself, it's been my experience that evangelicals view their time here on earth as a short layover in the grand scheme of things. Heaven is the final destination and things that concern us here on earth, such as social justice, are a distraction from the greater prize. Anything that takes away from the "personal relationship" with Jesus is viewed as a sin in itself. Social justice is seen as a distraction created by liberals who really don't believe in Jesus and heaven. At least that's what I was taught for many years.

For many of us who could consider ourselves post-evangelicals, we have changed our perspective from this time on earth as being a short layover to, instead, seeing it as a gift from our Creator. Social justice then is seen as an extension of our relationship with Jesus, not a distraction from it.

Phil Jackson

I will start off with a great quote from Medea Benjamin that explains what social justice is in order that you can judge for yourself and have a better position of understanding when people talk about it negatively.

Social justice means moving towards a society where all hungry are fed, all sick are cared for, the environment is treasured, and we treat each other with love and compassion. Not an easy goal, for sure, but certainly one worth giving our lives for!

Medea Benjamin is the co-founder of Global Exchange and Code Pink. Who better than followers of Jesus Christ to lead the world in understanding and living out the teachings of Jesus about social justice. One of the core reasons why evangelicals see the term so negatively is that the term has assumed baggage that has hurt the purity of the gospel. What people who take a negative view of the term "social justice" don't understand is that the gospel and social justice are one in the same. If you take either one away, the other is depleted of its power. Jesus taught to love your God with all your heart, soul, and mind, and to love your neighbor as yourself. This is the gospel and social justice all in one. He taught that whatever we do to the least of these is what we do to him! This is just what Medea stated, that social justice is moving toward a society where all are cared for, are treated equally, and treat each other with love and compassion.

Scriptural reference(s):

Matthew 22:34–40
Matthew 25:31–46
Matthew 28:11–15
Acts 11:24

Suggested additional sources:

- *Fear* by Joanna Bourke
- *Left, Right & Christ* by Lisa Sharon Harper and D.C. Innes
- *Love without Agenda* by Jimmy Spencer Jr.
- *With Justice for All* by John Perkins
- *The Post-Evangelical* by Dave Tomlinson
- *Everything Must Change: Jesus, Global Crises, and a Revolution of Hope* by Brian McLaren
- *Everyday Justice: The Global Impact of Our Daily Choices* by Julie Clawson
- www.everydayjustice.net
- www.goodandfairclothing.com
- www.Globalexchange.org

Questions for further discussion/thought:

1. Are there certain terms that, when you hear them, automatically bring about negative political thoughts of another people group?
2. What do you think it will take to undo the hate-filled rhetoric of contemporary political culture?
3. How does social justice fit into your theology?
4. Is our time here on earth a short layover, or is there something more to it? If so, what does that look like?

5. Can you have a personal relationship with Jesus and still believe in social justice?
6. What happens to a town, city, or country that does not practice social justice?

Source cited:

- *The Post-Evangelical* by Dave Tomlinson (El Cajon, Calif.: Zondervan/ Youth Specialties, 2003)

uestion

Many Christians read and study the King James Version of the Bible. Some believe it is the best and most accurate translation there is. Why? Can I read a different translation? What about paraphrases such as The Message?

Jonathan Brooks

A. Thou shalt comprehend thine manuscript as paramount as is achievable, and scrutinize the periphery in any manner thusly deemed appropriate. Translation: You can read whichever translation makes it easier for you to comprehend God's word.

Many Christians hold on to one translation even though they find themselves struggling for understanding. I believe the Bible is meant to be read and understood, so it is important that the individual reader finds a version he or she can read and understand. I also believe that the Bible was not written *to* us; it was written *for* us, meaning it was written to an ancient audience, and it is our responsibility to understand that but still use it in our modern culture. It is already difficult to understand some passages because of the cultural differences of our time. Reading paraphrases such as *The Message* and others can be helpful. Translators such as Eugene H. Peterson have gone through serious care to bring an ancient language to a modern audience. I would advise you to have as many translations as possible; this will help you gain different understandings of what the original writers were trying to convey.

Sean Gladding

Who is...
Sean Gladding

*I've had guns pointed at me
on more than one occasion.*

The way some people talk about the KJV, one could almost imagine that God should have chosen English for the original version. Its enduring popularity and revered status are quite remarkable given the awkwardness of the way it reads four centuries since it was translated. It was written in order to be read aloud in the liturgy of corporate worship, and the beauty of its poetry still moves us, much as Shakespeare can.

To state that it is the most accurate translation of scripture is to deny 400 years of the expansion of our understanding of both the Hebrew and Greek languages and the cultures out of which the Bible grew. Every translation is already an interpretation, as we choose which words to use from a range of possibilities. To pretend it is not is to be disingenuous. For instance, the translators of the KJV use "prince" for fourteen different Hebrew words. Coincidence? Or because the one paying for their services was King James? The impetus for this third English translation appears to have been the desire to reinforce the established institutional structure of the Church of England, which also no doubt shaped the language used.

When people ask me, "What translation of the Bible should I buy?" I invariably answer, "One you will actually read." This has meant that I often recommend *The Message* version, as it is so accessible for our culture. For me, the question is not which Bible to read, but how to read it. My conviction is that it is to be read in community with others, aloud and often—and then embody what we believe God is saying.

Phil Jackson

The King James Bible uses a linguistic style that no one currently identifies with, yet because of the elegant sound of the words, some folks believe that this is the way we have to talk when speaking to God. There's a lot of information out there about why the King James translation is not necessarily an accurate version of the Bible, and even more information from those who say it is the only version that should be read. So which is it?

If you cannot understand the Word of God, it means nothing. The purest way to read the Bible and to find its deep meaning is to read it in Hebrew, Greek, and/or Aramaic, but this is unrealistic for most of us, just trying to read English. So if you are going to spend time seeking truth from God's Word, find a version that is in a language that you are able to comprehend and to read easily, and go for it!

God is bigger than whatever version you choose, and yet He desires us to know Him though His word. Whether it's a paraphrase or the King James version, we must grow in our understanding of God, and that is best done when we are experiencing Him through His word.

Scriptural reference(s):

2 Timothy 2:15
2 Timothy 3:16
Hebrews 4:12

Suggested additional sources:

* *How to Read the Bible for All It's Worth* by Gordon Fee and Douglas Stewart
* *Eat This Book* by Eugene Peterson
* *Manna and Mercy* by Daniel Erlander
* *The Epic of Eden* by Sandra Richter
* *Scripture and the Authority of God: How to Read the Bible Today* by N. T. Wright
* *How to Read the Bible for All Its Worth* by Gordon D. Fee and Douglas Stuart

Questions for further discussion/thought:

1. Can you think of a time when you heard someone incorrectly and it ruined the relationship?
2. How important is it that you truly understand God's commands?
3. If you have read different translations, what was your experience in doing so?
4. What has been your experience of reading the Bible with other people?
5. How has that shaped the way you read the Bible today?
6. Why are there so many different versions of the Bible? Is one better or worse than the other?

7. Why do you think some churches use more than one translation, or even non-literal interpretations of the Bible?

Source cited:

- *The Holy Bible*

What does it actually mean when Christians say they believe that Jesus is the Son of God? And how, if at all, is this different from when other people are called "children of God"?

Matthew Paul Turner

Who is...
Matthew Paul Turner

Baking pies is one of my talents.

Although it is primarily applied to Jesus, the term "Son of God" pops up in other places where it isn't referring to Jesus (and we really wouldn't want it to). For example, in Genesis 6, the "sons of God" apparently thought that the "daughters of men" were hot, so they married them and had some sort of super-babies.

In the New Testament, the term is repeatedly applied to Jesus, and there is an implied exclusiveness to it. Part of the purpose of using this term appears to be subverting the claims of Rome and the Caesars. Beginning with Augustus, many of the Caesars applied the term "son of God" to themselves.

Of course, the most obvious meaning of Jesus as "the Son of God" has to do with the close connection between Jesus and the God he called "Father." This is more striking than it seems. Of the roughly 691 times the word for "father" occurs in the Old Testament, only 13 of them refer to God, and only two people dare to refer to God this way. In contrast, the word for "father" occurs roughly 388 times in the New Testament, and 250 of them refer directly to God, about half of them from Jesus. But, as soon as Jesus makes this seemingly exclusive connection, he deconstructs it, and refers to God as *our* Father. In Romans and Galatians, Paul goes on to make the scandalous claim that we have been adopted by God as his children and made co-heirs with Jesus. That isn't just theological jargon. It appears to be relational equality.

What does it mean when they say Jesus is the Son of God?

Phil Snider

It's remarkable how Christian language loses its edge as it's passed down through the centuries. In the early days of Christianity, calling Jesus the "Son of God" was a subversive act, bordering on treason. Why? For one very simple reason: in the Roman Empire, which represented the ruling order of the day, the son of God was Caesar, *not* Jesus. Yet in a sheer act of brilliance, the Christian narratives turned the table of the Roman Empire upside-down. To say that Jesus is the Son of God was to provocatively declare that Caesar is not.

Such rhetoric provided early Christian communities a way of reimagining how they believed God worked, no matter what the dominant powers in place tried to tell them. Is God revealed through brute displays of violence, as with Caesar, or through compassionate love, as with Jesus? Is God revealed through the love of power, as with Caesar, or through the power of love, as with Jesus? The answer to these questions meant the difference between life and death, in more ways than one. Perhaps it still does.

Doug Pagitt

The term "Son of God" was a title, not a description of a relationship. In other words, there is a difference in God's son and the Son of God.

For Jesus and his followers, the term Son of God was connected to the notion of the kingdom of God, which was rich with revolution. The Jews were a minority class under the rule of Rome, and Rome had a very powerful king, Caesar. Caesar declared himself a god. In fact, he declared that he should be referred to as "the son of God." The places in his territory where he was honored as a god were referred to as *ekklesia*, the Greek word that was later used by Christians to refer to the church. Around the empire there were communities that declared the kingdom of Caesar, the son of God, and met in ecclesia for that purpose.

When Jesus declared that the kingdom of God was at hand, it sat in direct contrast to the kingdom of Caesar. It was a political call of how people ought to live in the midst of their world. When the followers of Jesus declared him to be the Son of God, they were doing so in contrast to the claims of the followers of Caesar. This was revolutionary language. So to belong to the kingdom of God was the alternative to belonging to the kingdom of Caesar. This had poignant and dangerous implications.

Scriptural reference(s):

Mark 1:1
Mark 15:39

Suggested additional sources:

- *The First Christmas* by Marcus Borg and John Dominic Crossan
- *The Last Week* by Marcus Borg and John Dominic Crossan
- *Re-Imagine the World* by Bernard Brandon Scott

Questions for further discussion/thought:

1. How do most people today think God works? Do you think this is congruent with the way that God worked in the life of Jesus?
2. When it comes to calling Jesus the Son of God, do you think it is more helpful to do so (1) as a form of provocative rhetoric that challenges the dominant power structures of the day or (2) in terms of designating Jesus' divine status as a God?

Do all Christians believe Jesus died for their sins? What exactly does this mean, and where did the belief come from? If some Christians don't believe this, what do they believe about the crucifixion?

Bart Campolo

Who is...
Bart Campolo

I believe a global economic and social collapse of unprecedented proportions is imminent.

Actually, it has been a long time since I believed the cross, or the Resurrection for that matter, was necessary for our salvation. I know the apostle Paul thinks differently, but on this point I think the apostle Paul, and most of evangelical Christianity, are fundamentally wrong.

As far as I can tell, the essential message of evangelical Christianity is fairly simple: God wants to forgive us, but our sins are so terrible that God must first appease His sense of justice by killing somebody. Jesus, the Son of God, was born of a virgin so that God could kill him instead of us, once and for all, or at least for all who believe.

If I understand Jesus correctly, however, God wants the rest of us to just forgive each other. Not to exact retribution, not to demand compensation, certainly not to kill anybody. Just forgive, plain and simple. And if those same people sin against us again, we're supposed to forgive them again, over and over, out of the goodness of our hearts. You know, seventy times seven times, and all of that.

So, then, it seems to me that if almighty God himself really does want to forgive us, that God must be able to just forgive us in that same way, out of the goodness of God's own heart. At least that's what Jesus suggested when he taught his disciples to pray, "Forgive us our sins, as we forgive those who sin against us"—that is, plainly and simply, without killing anybody.

I don't think Jesus came to deliver us from God, but rather to share God's grace with us, so that we could be delivered from sin itself. God's grace, after all, is what gives us the confidence to overcome everything that is wrong with us, everything that keeps us from him and one another.

Of course, Jesus understood that grace always frightens and infuriates religious leaders, because the notion that God loves and forgives everybody no matter what they do or don't do evacuates the authority of such leaders and their rules. Indeed, Jesus clearly knew in advance that displaying and proclaiming God's grace would get him killed. Getting killed, however, was not the point.

Christian Piatt

In a word, no. The idea that Jesus died for humanity's sins is often called substitutionary atonement. For centuries following the life and death of Jesus, this was not central to the beliefs of many, if not most, Christians. Theologians such as Augustine of Hippo placed a strong emphasis on the salvific importance of the death of Jesus, but before that, most theological thinkers wrote about Jesus' life, death, and resurrection in terms that would suggest one was no more important than the other.

For me, the work of Walter Wink was essential to helping me articulate my position on this issue. His claim is that *violence never redeems*, but rather it is love that is redemptive. Now, some will argue that the sacrifice made by God and Jesus is the ultimate expression of love. Personally, I don't see much love in such a violent act.

Did God send Jesus to humanity? I believe so. Did we kill him? I believe we did. As such, it's my understanding that Jesus died *because of our sinfulness*, and because his message of radical love and justice posed such a threat to established power systems. His life embodied the notion of the end of justifiable violence. The way he lived and the way he died point the way for how humanity may find redemption from such darkness and violence.

I tend to believe that God cannot create any creature whose evil God cannot also bear and forgive. The idea of redemptive sacrifice is ancient, but I do not believe it is Christian.

Hugh Hollowell

In theological terms, you are asking about atonement theory, or, put simply, what did the death of Jesus mean or accomplish, if anything.

Believing that Jesus died for our sins, and thus somehow placated God, is a popular view of what the death of Jesus accomplished, but it is far from the only one.

173

Other popular views include the Christus Victor view (that by his death, Jesus overcame the work of the devil), the ransom view (that the death of Jesus somehow ransomed us from the devil) and my personal favorite, the moral example view (which says that Jesus was our example, and if you live a life like his, the powers that be will try to kill you, too).

So no, not everyone believes that the death of Jesus was all about his "dying for our sins." But that does not mean they aren't a Christian, or that the death of Jesus does not figure heavily in their faith.

Two Friars and a Fool

Who is...
Two Friars and a Fool

One of us is supposedly a world-traveling adventurer but ended up in the middle of nowhere, surrounded by the smell of processed beets.

In brief, no. Almost all Christians believe that Jesus' death was important, but even the Christians who say "Jesus died for our sins" mean different things. Looking into the past, there have been *at least* five big answers to the question of what Jesus' crucifixion meant:

1. God defeats Satan and Death by tricking them into killing Jesus, who then breaks out of hell, ending their dominion.
2. Jesus pays our cosmic sacrificial debt for moral failure, thus ransoming us out of captivity to sin, and claiming us for God.
3. God, constrained by holiness, must punish sinners, so Jesus takes the punishment on our behalf.
4. Jesus is the moral example who shows us a way of self-sacrificial living that leads to freedom, which God vindicates through resurrection.
5. God secures meaning for us even in experiences of extreme suffering through the presence of Jesus on the cross.

What strikes us is how incredibly boring and banal it would be if Jesus' death only meant one thing, or even only a few specific things. A person could just learn the "one true answer," memorize it, and stop thinking about it or struggling with it.

Leaders of God's people and government officials killed Jesus! Jesus was and is God! Jesus forgave them even in his death-throes! Jesus cried out that God had abandoned him! Jesus came back after that and ate fish!

Nothing about that is simple. You look to the cross, you come face to face with mystery. That's what makes this so fun.

Scriptural reference(s):

Matthew 5:38–48
John 3:16
Romans 8
Colossians 1:15–20

Suggested additional sources:

- *Jesus and Nonviolence: A Third Way* by Walter Wink
- *The Powers that Be* by Walter Wink
- *Love, Violence, and the Cross* by Gregory Anderson Love
- *Crucified God* by Jürgen Moltmann
- *Christus Victor: An Historical Study of the Three Main Types of the Idea of Atonement* by Gustav Aulén (trans. A. G. Hebert, SSM)

Questions for further discussion/thought:

1. Do you believe there can be salvation from sin without Jesus' blood being shed? Why or why not?
2. How do we reconcile this idea of God sending his Son to be sacrificed with the idea of an all-loving, all-merciful God?
3. Consider a famous movie, poem, or painting. Can it be reduced to a single interpretation or meaning, or does it have enough depth to support various readings?
4. Have you ever encountered an explanation of Jesus' crucifixion—and why it is important—which left unanswered questions, or didn't satisfy? What was the explanation, and why wasn't it satisfactory?
5. Looking above at five major things that Christians throughout history have said about the importance and meaning of Jesus' death on the cross, do you have a favorite? Is there one or more you've never heard before?

Source cited:

- *Jesus and Nonviolence: A Third Way* by Walter Wink (Minneapolis: Fortress, 2003)

Christian Piatt

Who is...
Christian Piatt

My middle name is Damien.

A. Historically, Christianity has been structured in a way that the leader or leaders are afforded a great amount of power, trust, and latitude over the rest of the community. This began in earnest with Catholicism, and, from there, has made its way into nearly every expression of the Christian Church ever since.

Consider this: wherever there is a combination of largely unchecked power, and profound trust, there will be abuses of that power. It's part of the inevitable "shadow side" of human nature. This doesn't mean that Christianity itself breeds such exploitation and abuse, but it is fertile ground for those who might seek a context in which they can prey on others' vulnerabilities.

Part of what people such as Martin Luther, Barton Stone, and Alexander Campbell sought to do was wrest such power from figures of authority, removing the necessity for a mediator between people and God. Once we do not lean on another person, clergy or otherwise, to connect us to God, that power and the potential for its abuse is greatly reduced.

It doesn't mean that there aren't still examples of such exploitation. Sometimes we are so desperate for meaning or belonging that we'll endow others with far more trust than they deserve. But even in light of this potential risk, it doesn't mean that we don't still need one another.

It is in community that our joys are multiplied and our suffering is diluted. But that doesn't require divestment of authority onto another; it requires accountability and love.

Matthew Paul Turner

A. Belief is a powerful reality for people. Many of us seek to make our faith the core of who we are, the entity that shapes and defines the deepest parts of our being. That's why, for so many people, faith is an influential source of hope and peace and change in their lives. But pursuing the unseen also makes some of us emotionally and mentally vulnerable to being led "astray" by dynamic people, wolves dressed up like lambs, who proclaim to know the true "Christianity" or a "secret" about faith in God.

Cult leaders don't usually begin with what is different or unique about their "faith in God." They almost always lead with what they have in common with a would-be convert. From those common foundations, narcissistic (and sometimes clinically insane) "pastors" are able to build a trust with a group of people, a trust that begins to shape and mold the deepest parts of who these people are and slowly, over time, form a bond that is emotionally and spiritually codependent. Sooner or later, those innocent, vulnerable Christians become so involved, so brainwashed that their "shepherds" are able to lead them into all kinds of ugly spiritual realities.

Thankfully, most cults never end up turning into Jonestown scenarios. But since most Christian cults don't pursue Jonestown-style mass congregational suicides, or other headline-grabbing stunts, a lot of them go unnoticed.

Faith is a powerful tool, one that can be used to spring forth hope and one that can be wielded to manipulate, harm, and lead large and small groups of people into spiritually unhealthy realities.

Phil Snider

Who is...
Phil Snider

I wrote my last two responses for this book
while my eleven-year-old son fell asleep listening
to his Beatles playlist on repeat, and I was
too lazy to go upstairs and turn it off.

I vividly remember sitting in theology class on the morning of September 13, 2001. It was the first time we had met after the tragedies that struck just two days before. Like so many others, I was feeling a mixture of sadness and shock. Even when I look back on things now, everything remains so surreal.

Our professor looked at us that morning and, with sadness in his voice, made a simple yet profound statement that has stayed with me ever since: "What happened on Tuesday is an example of horrific moral evil done by those claiming to know the mind of God."

His point was that anytime human beings claim to have the God's-eye view of the world, dangerous things are likely to happen, whether in New York City or Oklahoma City. This is why fundamentalism of any stripe is dangerous, whether it be Christian, Muslim, Jewish, or whatever.

Dangerous cults, in typical fundamentalist fashion, are fueled by an unhealthy combination of anger and fear, which cultic leaders draw upon in order to tell followers who is to blame. They use religion to justify their claims, for what higher authority is there than God?

Perhaps our world would be a little better off if we didn't view God as the authority that legitimizes our perspectives but rather as the disturbance that undoes our perspectives. Instead of claiming to speak for God, perhaps religion should remind us that speaking for God is precisely what we are unable to do.

Scriptural reference(s):

Genesis 11:1–9

Suggested additional sources:

- *Malignant Pied Pipers of Our Time: A Psychological Study of Destructive Cult Leaders from Rev. Jim Jones to Osama bin Laden* by Peter A. Olsson, M.D.
- www.howcultswork.com
- *When Religion Becomes Evil* by Charles Kimball
- *Belief* by Gianni Vattimo

Questions for further discussion/thought:

1. What is the difference to you between a healthy faith community and a cult?
2. Do you think there's something unique about Christianity that gives rise to so many cults?
3. Why do you think Christian ethicists throughout the centuries have reminded us not to treat evil as if it is something entirely outside of ourselves?
4. If it's not possible to know the absolute mind of God, then what is the starting point for Christian ethics? In other words, how do we determine how to act responsibly?

Contributor List, Bios, and Suggested Resources

Contributor: Adam J. Copeland

Professional title: Faculty Director for Faith and Leadership, Concordia College, Moorhead, Minnesota

Personal website(s), email, blog, podcast, etc.:
A Wee Blether, http://adamjcopeland.com
Twitter: @ajc123

Bio: Adam J. Copeland is Faculty Director for Faith and Leadership at Concordia College in Moorhead, Minnesota, where he teaches in the department of religion. He has served as pastor of a rural Presbyterian congregation and mission developer of a Lutheran emergent ministry. Among other publications, Adam's writing has appeared in *The Christian Century*, *WorkingPreacher.org*, *The Huffington Post*, and in several books. He is associate editor of *Journal for Preachers*, and his broad interests include Christian ministry, digital religion, emerging church, and practical theology. An ordained minister in the Presbyterian Church (USA), Adam holds degrees from St. Olaf College and Columbia Theological Seminary. To read more of Adam's writing visit *A Wee Blether* (http://adamjcopeland.com) and follow his tweets @ajc123.

Recommended books, websites, blogs, and other resources for people to explore:

www.TheThoughtfulChristian.com
Amazing Grace: A Vocabulary of Faith by Kathleen Norris
Keeping the Faith in Seminary by Ellie Roscher
Everything by Barbara Brown Taylor
Rachel Held Evan's blog, http://rachelheldevans.com/
Julie Clawson's blog, http://julieclawson.com/
Bruce Reyes Chow's blog, http://www.patheos.com/blogs/breyeschow/

Favorite quote:

I hate quotable quotes.

—Adam Copeland

Five things people can do today, in their own community, to help make the world a better place:

1. Get to know a person of another faith.
2. Pray.
3. Read a local newspaper—I know, shocking—to gain local awareness.
4. Use Facebook and other social media to spread love, not snark.
5. Host a block party.

Contributor: Andrew Marin

Professional title: President and Founder of The Marin Foundation
Personal website(s), email, blog, podcast, etc.:
  Website: www.themarinfoundation.org
  Blog: www.loveisanorientation.com
  Twitter: @Andrew_Marin
  Facebook: facebook.com/marin.andrew
Bio: Andrew Marin is the President and Founder of The Marin Foundation, a nonprofit organization working to build bridges between the LGBT community and theological and political conservatives. He is the author of the award-winning book *Love Is an Orientation* (2009) and its interactive DVD curriculum (2011), and has been featured on a number of media outlets including the BBC World News, NPR, ABC, and CBS, among others. Since 2010 Andrew has advised various agencies of the United Nations and the U.S. government on issues of faith, sexuality and cultural aspects of reconciliation. He has an M.A. in Urban Studies with concentrations in Social Change and Theology from Eastern University, and lives in Chicago's LGBT neighborhood, Boystown, with his wife Brenda.

Recommended books, websites, blogs, and other resources for people to explore:

Friendship at the Margins by Chris Heuertz and Christine Pohl
Love without Agenda by Jimmy Spencer Jr.
www.redletterchristians.org

Favorite quotes:

It's the Holy Spirit's job to convict, God's job to judge, and my job to love.
                                                                    —Billy Graham

Hope is a shield that provides space to continue moving forward.
—Andrew Marin

I am not afraid of the word tension. I have earnestly opposed violent tension my whole life; but there is a type of constructive, nonviolent tension which produces growth.
—Martin Luther King Jr.

We will stop failing when we stop trying to succeed and start establishing kingdom.
—Andrew Marin

Faithfulness wins 100% of the time.
—Andrew Marin

Being faithful is success. If other successes come from that, then that is a blessing.
—Mother Teresa

Five things people can do today, in their own community, to help make the world a better place:

1. Google your "city's name" and the word "*gay*" and see what pops up. When you find an organization, group, meeting, etc., show up to listen and learn.
2. Set up a meeting in which you intentionally bring together a progressive LGBT person and a straight conservative Christian. The three of you then have a conversation in which everyone can actually hear each other instead of just reading activist generalizations on the Internet and forming false opinions.
3. Attend an LGBT church and set up a meeting with the pastor afterward to reflect on your experience. Or if you are more progressive, do the opposite with a conservative evangelical church and pastor.
4. Find the greatest amount of suffering in your local community causing legitimate reasons to question God, and then go and serve the afflicted group for no other reason than being compelled by Jesus to do good.
5. There is an overemphasized need to listen to what other people in authority positions (e.g., pastors, authors) have to say about God and the Bible. Go buy a Bible commentary book and use it to help you read the entire Bible from cover to cover, trying to answer your own questions instead of always turning to other people. After you have done that, feel free to turn to others in your community for further discussion and exploration.

Contributor: Bart Campolo

Professional title: Director of Outreach, the Telos Group
Personal website(s), email, blog, podcast, etc.:
  www.thewalnuthillsfellowship.org
  www.telosgroup.org
Bio: Bart Campolo is a veteran urban minister and activist who speaks and
  writes about faith, loving relationships, and social justice. Bart is the
  leader of The Walnut Hills Fellowship, a small faith community in inner-
  city Cincinnati, and the founder of Mission Year, a Christian ministry that
  recruits committed young adults to live and work among the poor in inner-
  city neighborhoods across the country.

  Born and raised in suburban Philadelphia, Bart graduated from Brown
  University in 1985, after which he worked with young people in South
  Minneapolis, where he met and married his wife, Marty. In 1989 the
  Campolos moved to West Philadelphia to found Kingdomworks, the urban
  ministry that later became Mission Year, and to begin raising their children,
  Miranda and Roman, who are now young adults.

  In 2005, after nearly two decades of organizational leadership, the
  Campolo family moved from Philadelphia to the Walnut Hills neighborhood
  of Cincinnati, to love their neighbors in a more personal way. Bart now
  works in collaboration with the Telos Group and others, educating America's
  mainstream faith leaders and their communities about the causes of, and
  solutions to, the modern conflict that currently ravages the Holy Land.

Recommended books, websites, blogs, and other resources for people to explore:

When Bad Things Happen to Good People by Harold Kushner

Favorite quote:

*The penalty of deception is to become a deception, with all sense of moral
distinction vitiated. A man who lies habitually becomes a lie, and it is increasingly impossible for him to know when he is lying and when he is not.*
                                                              —Howard Thurman

Five things people can do today, in their own community, to help make the world a better place:

1. Invite a lonely person to dinner.
2. Clean up the trash on your street.

3. Eat (not volunteer) at the local soup kitchen.
4. Plant a vegetable garden.
5. Use public transportation.

Contributor: Brian Ammons

Professional title: Chaplain and Director of Spiritual Life, Warren Wilson College

Bio: Brian Ammons is a pastor, educator, and spiritual director who lives and works in Asheville, NC. Brian hold a PhD in Curriculum and Cultural Studies from UNC-Greensboro, a MDiv from Wake Forest University, and a MEd in Special Education from UNC-Charlotte. He is passionate about working with young people at the intersection of spirituality, justice, and education— particularly as it relates to rethinking the possibilities of identity construction.

Recommended books, websites, blogs, and other resources for people to explore:

Radical Love: An Introduction to Queer Theology by Patrick Cheng
Anything ever written by Marcella Althaus Reid

Favorite quote:

"I'm gonna cause you a miracle
when you see the way I kept God's image alive.

Forgiveness
is for anybody
who needs a safe passage through my mind."
                    —Buddy Wakefield, Hurling Crowbirds at Mockingbars

Five things people can do today, in their own community, to help make the world a better place:

1. Talk to your neighbor.
2. Adopt a dog.
3. Write a letter to thank your favorite teacher.
4. Be nice to folks who stand behind counters for a living.
5. Advocate for comprehensive sex education!!!

Contributor: Carol Howard Merritt

Professional title: Author and Speaker
Personal website(s), email, blog, podcast, etc.:
    www.TribalChurch.org
    www.GodComplexRadio.com
    Twitter: @CarolHoward
    carolhowardmerritt@gmail.com
Bio: Carol Howard Merritt grew up along the beach in Florida. After being
    raised as a conservative Baptist and attending a fundamentalist Bible
    college, she went to seminary and decided to become a minister. Carol has
    been a pastor for 12 years, serving Presbyterian Churches in the swamps
    of Cajun Louisiana, a bayside village in Rhode Island, and in an urban
    neighborhood in D.C. She is the author of *Tribal Church* (Alban, 2007)
    and *Reframing Hope* (Alban, 2010) and contributed to *The Hyphenateds*
    by Phil Snider (Chalice Press, 2011). She is a frequent contributor to the
    Christian Century and the *Huffington Post*. She blogs at TribalChurch.org
    and cohosts God Complex Radio, a podcast with Derrick Weston. Carol
    lives in Chattanooga, Tennessee, with her daughter and husband, Brian
    Merritt, who is starting a new church. You can follow her on Twitter @
    CarolHoward.

Recommended books, websites, blogs, and other resources for people to explore:

Tribal Church by Carol Howard Merritt
Reframing Hope by Carol Howard Merritt
www.TribalChurch.org
www.HuffingtonPost.com/Religion/

Favorite quote:

If you love it enough, anything will talk with you.
                                        —George Washington Carver

Five things people can do today, in their own community, to help make the world a better place:

1. Work in a women's shelter, family shelter, or soup kitchen in a capacity
    so that we build relationships with the guests. As we do, we can
    remember that a society is only as strong as its weakest members.

2. Develop and sustain local economies. Buying our food at farmers' markets and shopping at the mom and pop store not only help our neighbors have more meaningful employment, but it is better for the environment.
3. Celebrate creativity. A society will produce and reflect those things that are celebrated. If a community reveres greed and poor treatment of workers, then it will increase the gap between the rich and the poor. If we celebrate artists, through attending exhibits, showing up at concerts, reading books, and buying hand-crafted goods, then we will produce artists.
4. Fight for equality in education. The education of each child in our community is important, and a kid should not receive an excellent or poor education depending on which block that child lives. Talk to a teacher or do some research on the Internet. Learn which schools are failing and work to close the education gap.
5. Rip up the lawn. Enormous amounts of water and chemicals are spent keeping these green rugs in front of our homes pristine. What can we do instead? Can we begin to grow vegetable gardens? Are there plants that are native to our area that will thrive without continued maintenance?

Contributor: Christian Piatt

Professional title: Author/Speaker/Blogger
Personal website(s), email, blog, podcast, etc.:
   www.christianpiatt.com
   www.patheos.com/blogs/christianpiatt/
Bio: Christian is the creator and editor of the Banned Questions book series. He has written, edited, and contributed to a number of books on faith and culture, young adult spirituality, and postmodern theology. His memoir, *PregMANcy: A Dad, a Little Dude and a Due Date*, takes an irreverent and deeply personal look at the male experience of pregnancy, childbirth, and fatherhood.

   Christian's next book, called *postChristian*, about the role of Christ followers in a post-Christendom culture, will be published in hardcover in summer 2014.

Recommended books, websites, blogs, and other resources for people to explore:

Jesus and Nonviolence: A Third Way by Walter Wink
The Powers that Be by Walter Wink

The Weakness of God by John Caputo
Insurrection by Peter Rollins

Favorite quotes:

Be the change you want to see in the world.

—Mahatma Gandhi

If there is a problem and there is something you can do about it, don't worry about it; if there is a problem and there is nothing you can do about it, don't worry about it.

—Buddhist proverb

Truly, I say to you, as you did it to one of the least of these my brothers, you did it to me.

—Matthew 25:40, ESV

Five things people can do today, in their own community, to help make the world a better place:

1. Listen more; talk less.
2. Care daily for your mind, body, and spirit. An imbalanced schedule leads to an imbalanced life.
3. Give more than you think you can afford, and accept less than you think you deserve.
4. Know where the things you buy come from. One of your most powerful tools is in your wallet.
5. Pray for wisdom, peace, clarity, and courage, but do not hold God accountable for your personal expectations.

Contributor: Doug Pagitt

Professional title: Pastor, Author, Speaker, Radio Show Host, and Social Media Business Owner
Personal website(s), email, blog, podcast, etc.:
www.DougPagitt.com
www.DougPagittRadio.com
www.SolomonsPorch.com
www.EmergentVillage.com

Bio: I'm a pastor, author, speaker, radio show host, and social media business owner living in Minneapolis, Minnesota. I'm married to Shelley Pagitt and am the parent to four young adult children. I'm part of Emergent Village. I'm the pastor of Solomon's Porch in Minneapolis.

Recommended books, websites, blogs, and other resources for people to explore:

http://www.scientificamerican.com - Look at it every week
Pathos.com/blogs/EmergentVillage
www.DougPagittRadio.com

Favorite quote:

It ain't what you don't know that get's you into trouble; It's what you know for sure that just ain't so.

—Mark Twain

Five things people can do today, in their own community, to help make the world a better place:

1. Become friends with those with whom you disagree.
2. Tell stories of the light of God you see in other people.
3. Buy or bring a lunch for someone you work with once a week.
4. Kiss a baby.
5. Ask someone every week how they think the world could be made better.

Contributor: Hugh Hollowell

Professional title: Reverend. I am the Pastor and Executive Director at Love Wins Ministries
Personal website(s), email, blog, podcast, etc.: I blog for work at www.lovewinsministries.org and personally at www.hughlh.com
Bio: Hugh Hollowell is a minister in the Mennonite Church USA and is based in Raleigh, N.C. He is the founder and director of Love Wins Ministries, which tackles the problems of homelessness by focusing on relationships, not outcomes. Hugh lives in downtown Raleigh with his wife, two cats and four chickens. He likes peanut M&Ms.

Recommended books, websites, blogs, and other resources for people to explore:

www.lovewinsministries.org

Favorite quotes:

I don't have a ministry; I have a life.

—Rev. Will D. Campbell

We have all known the long loneliness and we have learned that the only solution is love and that love comes with community.

—Dorothy Day

Five things people can do today, in their own community, to help make the world a better place:

1. Love your neighbor.
2. Learn the names of your geographic neighbors.
3. Learn how to ask for help.
4. When in doubt, do the most relational thing.
5. Recognize that everyone has has a voice, but not everyone has always been heard.

Contributor: Jonathan E. L. Brooks

Professional title: Senior Pastor of Canaan Community Church
Personal website(s), email, blog, podcast, etc.:
   www.canaancommunitychurch.org
   info@canaancommunitchurch.org
   www.facebook.com/canaancommunitychurch
   Twitter: @CanaanLoveGP
Bio: Jonathan Brooks is the Senior Pastor of Chicago-based Canaan Community Church and the CEO of Canaan Community Redevelopment Corporation (CCRC). These two entities and various partnerships provide for youth development, holistic health options, affordable housing, alternative education options, and re-entry assistance for ex-offenders in the West Englewood community.

   Jonathan has also been an elementary teacher for Chicago Public Schools for nine years, and he is on the front line of sustainable education reform in Chicago. He is currently enrolled at Northern Seminary, pursuing his Master of Divinity in Christian Community Development.

Under the name of Amen Anointed, he has recorded four hip-hop albums with the group Out-World, and he is working on his first solo project titled "Can I Get an Amen."

Jonathan and his wife, Michéal, have two beautiful girls, Jasmine and Jade, and reside just a few blocks away from the church campus.

Recommended books, websites, blogs, and other resources for people to explore:

Black and Free by Tom Skinner
Let Justice Roll Down by John Perkins
Preaching with Sacred Fire: An Anthology of African American Sermons

Favorite quotes:

Darkness cannot drive out darkness, only light can do that. Likewise, hate cannot drive out hate, only love can do that.

—Martin Luther King Jr.

I speak to the black experience, but I am always talking about the human condition—about what we can endure, dream, fail at, and still survive.

—Maya Angelou

There is no power on earth that can neutralize the influence of a high, simple and useful life.

—Booker T. Washington

Five things people can do today, in their own community, to help make the world a better place:

1. Plant a community garden and share the fresh food with neighbors.
2. Adopt a local school and volunteer regularly.
3. Get with a local artist and do beautification projects with youth.
4. Start a block club and a neighborhood watch or community policing group.
5. "Share the gospel at all times, and when necessary use words" (attributed to St. Francis).

Contributor: Margot Starbuck

Professional title: Author and Speaker
Personal website(s), email, blog, podcast, etc.:
www.MargotStarbuck.com
Bio: Margot Starbuck, a graduate of Westmont College and Princeton
Seminary, is passionate about communicating to individuals—in print
and in speech—the promise that God, in Jesus Christ, is with them and
for them. Margot's first book, *The Girl in the Orange Dress*, was awarded
the Advanced Writers and Speakers Association's best nonfiction book
of the year for 2011. Margot blogs for Red Letter Christians, Sojo, Gifted
for Leadership, FullFill, and Her.meneutics. She is the confessions editor
for *Geez Magazine*'s Sinner's Corner. (Awesome, right?) Margot enjoys
connecting with audiences on campuses, at conferences, festivals, and the
occasional adult living facility.

At home in Durham, North Carolina, with her husband and three
children by birth and adoption, Margot hangs out with teens and adults
who live with disabilities through Reality Ministries.

Recommended books, websites, blogs, and other resources for people to explore:

The Inner Voice of Love by Henri Nouwen – I absolutely love this book; if
you've got issues to work through, this is your companion
The Definitive Book of Body Language – also a big fan of this one…
fascinating!
http://www.christianitytoday.com/thisisourcity/7thcity/building-a-
beloved-community.html – this is my sweet new neighborhood
www.RealityMinistriesInc.org – God-breathed things happening in
Durham, N.C.

Favorite quote:

*There are people in the world so hungry that God cannot appear to them except
in the form of bread.*

—Mahatma Gandhi

Five things people can do today, in their own community, to help make the world a better place:

1. Share coffee with someone from a different faith tradition. They may
not go to your church, but with any luck you can wrangle some up in

your neighborhood, school, or workplace. (That was facetious. Don't be a user.)

2. Whatever your view on either the ordination or submission of women, engage in conversation with someone who holds an opposing position. Pay such close attention that you can articulate it without smirking, eye-rolling, or giggling.

3. Purpose to cross a language barrier in your community. Whether your neighbors use American Sign Language, or Spanish, or Hebrew, take a courageous risk to meet your neighbors where they are.

4. If you're straight, invite a gay couple or family to dinner. (As with #1, don't be a user. Just treat folks like…you treat folks.)

5. If you're a person of affluence—be honest, book-reader!—sponsor a child through Compassion International. Through this remarkable ministry, God is setting free the poor and the rich in one fell swoop. It's a win, people.

Contributor: Matthew Paul Turner

Personal website(s), email, blog, podcast, etc.:
   Email MatthewPaulTurner@gmail.com
   Blog: MatthewPaulTurner.net
   Twitter: @JesusNeedsNewPR
   Facebook: Facebook.com/MatthewPaulTurner
   Pinterest: Pinterest.com/mpt
   Podcast: 9Thumbs.com
Bio: Matthew Paul Turner is a blogger, speaker and author of nearly 20 books including *Churched, Hear No Evil* and *The Coffeehouse Gospel*. He is also a passionate advocate for World Vision. Before he began writing and speaking full-time, he served as editor of *CCM* and music and entertainment editor of Crosswalk.com. He and his wife, Jessica, along with their two kids, live in Nashville, Tenn.

Recommended books, websites, blogs, and other resources for people to explore:

One Thousand Gifts by Ann Voskamp
Praying for Strangers by River Jordan
Any book by Henri Nouwen
McSweeneys.net
TentMaker.org

Favorite quotes:

You can safely assume you've created God in your own image when it turns out that God hates all the same people you do.
— Anne Lamott

Somewhere we know that without silence words lose their meaning, that without listening speaking no longer heals, that without distance closeness cannot cure.
— Henri J.M. Nouwen

The Christian ideal has not been tried and found wanting; it has been found difficult and left untried.
— G.K. Chesterton

Five things people can do today, in their own community, to help make the world a better place:

1. Know their (actual) neighbors. Too many of us live isolated and unknown in the spaces we call home.
2. Vote Democrat? Kidding. But do vote. Participating in the political conversation is one of those ugly necessary actions that many of us do not engage.
3. Coach a community children's team. Investing in the lives of our community's children is one way we can leave a lasting legacy.
4. Recycle. It's a huge pain in the butt. But it showcases care and concern for God's creation.
5. Sit out on your front porch. Engage in conversations with the people who pass. God might just make your front porch a community gathering place.

Contributor: Phil Jackson

Professional title: Pastor Phil
Personal website(s), email, blog, podcast, etc.:
   www.thafirehouse.org
   www.thahouse.org
Bio: Kim's husband, a dad, a son, follower of Jesus. Founder/Pastor of The House Covenant Church, a Christ-centered, hip-hop worship. Founder/President of The Firehouse Community Art Center. Seeks to communicate love, grace, and justice to youth and young adults in the city.

Recommended books, websites, blogs, and other resources for people to explore:

The Hip-Hop Church: Connecting with the Movement Shaping Our Culture by Efrem Smith and Phil Jackson

Can't Stop Won't Stop: A History of the Hip-Hop Generation by Jeff Chang and D.J. Kool Herc

www.holyculture.net

Reflecting Black: African-American Cultural Criticism by Michel Eric Dyson (American culture)

Hip Hop America by Nelson George

Hip Hop Generation: Young Blacks and the Crisis in African American Culture by Bakari Kitwana

Black Noise: Rap Music and Black Culture in Contemporary America by Tricia Rose (music culture)

Favorite quote:

Less definition of the Gospel and more demonstration.

—Phil Jackson

Five things people can do today, in their own community, to help make the world a better place:

1. Pick up the trash from your community. Everyday just walk around with a trash can picking up trash. Your community will notice and gradually follow.
2. Know the names of your neighbors. know who they are, what they like. Invite them over for BBQ. Be a neighbor to your neighbors.
3. Support your local public schools by volunteering to serve them. Help at games, with security in school, in after-school tutoring, with coaching a team, or in class rooms with teachers! Just being a caring adult to a young person is key!
4. Find a senior and learn from him or her. This could occur at a nursing home, church, anywhere, but learn by spending time talking with the individual. See if there are some other young people you could find to sit with the person as well, and let the person teach you.
5. Find a youth, young adult, someone a little younger than you, and commit to investing your time, talent and even loot with them in order that they will learn from your mistakes and grow in Christ, understanding of life and in how to merge all of that in to a strong life!

Contributor: Phil Shepherd, *a.k.a.* The Whiskey Preacher

Professional title: Rev. Philip E. Shepherd

Personal website(s), email, blog, podcast, etc.:

www.whiskeypreacher.com

www.philshepherd.com

Bio: Phil Shepherd (A.K.A. The Whiskey Preacher) is a native of Anchorage, Alaska. He has lived and pastored from that extreme corner of the continent to the other extreme corner known as Florida. In between these extremes, Phil has resided in Vancouver, B.C.; Minneapolis, Minnesota; and most recently in Fort Worth, Texas, where he and his beautiful, wicked-smart wife Stephanie (who is his co-pastor) planted The Eucatastrophe in the fall of 2007.

Entering his eighteenth year of ministry, Phil is a proud husband, mourning son, stubborn brother, uncle to teenagers, Alaskan grown, Texan transplant, an outlaw theologian, queer inclusive, friend of emergent, third cousin of Johnny Cash, writer, speaker, consultant, hater of human trafficking, foul-mouthed (as appropriate) , tattoo lover, cigar smoker, and connoisseur of various whiskies… Phil is the Whiskey Preacher.

Recommended books, websites, blogs, and other resources for people to explore:

Fast Company magazine

Wired magazine

Traveling Mercies by Anne Lamott

The Hunger Games Trilogy by Suzanne Collins

The Girl with the Dragon Tattoo Trilogy by Stieg Larsson

www.knightopia.com – Steve Knight's blog

Favorite quotes:

The church is a whore, but she is still my mother.

—Carol Jung

I don't give a f*#! what you have to say if you don't give back to the community.

—Becky Holmes (The Eucatastrophe intern)

Five things people can do today, in their own community, to help make the world a better place:

1. Authenticity in a faith community can be scary and messy, yet it is one of the healthiest things that can be implemented into the life of a church.
2. Embracing change does not have to take away from the rich history of your church; the changes you embrace today will help build on the richness of your history of yesteryears.
3. Let love for the Creator and love for the creation be the ultimate guide for your personal faith journey as well as your faith community.
4. Always be moldable; remember that you are the clay and God is the potter; God is the ultimate artisan and has creative dreams for your journey.
5. As Christians, we at times buy into the myth that life is supposed to be roses and Justin Bieber concerts, but in reality life can be hell here on earth...especially if you like good music. This is why, I believe, God did not create us to travel alone, so we can endure the bad times together and celebrate the good times together...even if we don't have Bieber fever.

Contributor: Phil Snider

Professional title: Writer, Speaker, Pastor, or The Rev. Dr. Phil Snider
Personal website(s), email, blog, podcast, etc.:
    www.philsnider.net
    philsnider@gmail.com
Bio: Phil Snider is a pastor at Brentwood Christian Church (Disciples of Christ) in Springfield, Missouri. His books include *Preaching After God: Derrida, Caputo, and the Language of Postmodern Homiletics*; *Toward a Hopeful Future: Why the Emergent Church Is Good News for Mainline Congregations* (winner of the 2011 Mayflower Award); and *The Hyphenateds: How Emergence Christianity is Re-Traditioning Mainline Practices*. He is a graduate of Missouri State University, Phillips Theological Seminary, and Chicago Theological Seminary.

Recommended books, websites, blogs, and other resources for people to explore:

www.peterrollins.net
http://katharinesarahmoody.tumblr.com/
www.kesterbrewin.com

www.blakehuggins.com
Insurrection: To Believe Is Human; to Doubt Divine by Peter Rollins
*Razing Hell: Rethinking Everything You've Been Taught About God's Wrath and
    Judgment* by Sharon Baker
The Weakness of God by John Caputo

Favorite quotes:

Let your religion be less of a theory and more of a love affair.
                                                        —G. K. Chesterton

Sometimes you have to stand up for what you believe you're not sure about.
                                                        —George Carlin

*What is a poet? An unhappy person who conceals profound anguish in his
heart but whose lips are so formed that as sighs and cries pass over them they
sound like beautiful music.*
                                                        —Søren Kierkegaard

Five things people can do today, in their own community, to help make the world a better place:

1. Start a garden and donate half of the healthy, freshly grown produce to a local food pantry.
2. Become an active participant in a local PFLAG group, or begin one if your community doesn't have one.
3. On a monthly basis, have dinner with someone who practices a different religion than you.
4. If you're not a vegetarian, refuse to eat factory farmed meat.
5. Drive less, bike more.

Contributor: Sean Gladding

Professional title: Author
Personal website(s), email, blog, podcast, etc.:
    www.seangladding.com
Bio: Sean is the author of *The Story of God, the Story of Us* (IVP, 2010), which
    is the written form of a narrative introduction to the Bible that he and his
    wife Rebecca have been leading people through for a decade, and which
    has now been told on six continents. He is papa to Maggie and Seth. He
    grew up in Norwich, England, and is a long-distance fan of his hometown
    team, the Canaries.

He was the first person in his family to begin to follow Jesus. He has lived in the United States for 20 years: 14 years in Texas and 6 in Kentucky. He is a founding member of Communality, a missional community in Lexington, Kentucky. He co-pastored a church in Houston called Mercy Street, a community made up of people wounded by the church or wrestling with addiction—often both. He aspires to be a Christian.

Recommended books, websites, blogs, and other resources for people to explore:

The Big Book of Alcoholics Anonymous
The Challenge of Jesus by N. T. Wright (and pretty much everything else he
    has written)
Life Together by Dietrich Bonhoeffer
Life of the Beloved by Henri Nouwen
The Ragamuffin Gospel by Brennan Manning
The Violence of Love by Archbishop Oscar Romero
The Christ of the Mount by E. Stanley Jones
Salvation Means Creation Healed by Howard Snyder
Colossians Remixed by Brian J. Walsh and Sylvia Keesmaat
Serve God, Save the Planet by Matthew Sleeth
The Jesus Storybook Bible by Sally Lloyd-Jones and Jago
Skallagrigg by William Horwood (my favorite novel)
http://rachelheldevans.com/blog
http://www.jrdkirk.com/

Favorite quotes:

Act justly, love mercy, and walk humbly with your God.
                                                    —The prophet Micah

Trust God. Clean house. Serve others.
                                                    —Alcoholics Anonymous

Got to kick at the darkness till it bleeds daylight.
                                                    —Bruce Cockburn

Some people care too much. I think it's called love.
                                                    —Winnie the Pooh

If you meet more than two assholes in a day, you're one of them.

—Clay E.

It may be that when we no longer know which way to go that we have come to our real journey. The mind that is not baffled is not employed. The impeded stream is the one that sings.

—Wendell Berry

My dad can't vote because he's a zombie.

—Maggie, age 6 (I am, in fact, a resident alien.)

Five things people can do today, in their own community, to help make the world a better place:

1. Sit on your front porch and not your back deck.
2. Start a neighborhood potluck dinner.
3. Plant gardens not lawns.
4. Support local businesses rather than national chains.
5. Make amends promptly when you hurt someone.

Contributor: Two Friars and a Fool

Professional title: Proprietary Theologians of an Imaginary Pub
Personal website(s), email, blog, podcast, etc.:
  http://twofriarsandafool.com
  God Complex Radio contributors
  Losing Your Religion guests
  @TwoFriars
  @AndAFool
  http://facebook.com/twofriarsandafool
Bio: Two Friars and a Fool is the result of a heady mix of alcohol, sleep deprivation, and the kind of hubris that makes blogging seem like a good way to contribute to society.

   Aric Clark is religious but not spiritual, and inflicts that religion on a congregation in Fort Morgan, Colorado. He is an over-functioning Enneagram 8, shouting at the universe from his pulpit.

   Doug Hagler is a deep-water Facebook argument-trawler who wants to open up the canon and add the collected works of J.R.R. Tolkien. As a fatbeard-at-large in North Amish-Land, Ohio, he lives out his calling to design role-playing games and write things on the Internet while pretending to actually work.

Nick Larson is a post-doctrinal, postmodern hipster who messes it all up by wearing Star Wars shirts non-ironically. He is always reading every book he can find with the word "Toward" in the title, and he is currently teaching rock-paper-scissors-lizard-Spock to disciples in Columbia, Missouri.

These three invite friends and dissidents to post brilliant articles on www.twofriarsandafool.com and then ruin them with their video responses. They tell themselves that only one of them is the Fool, but they are wrong.

Recommended books, websites, blogs, and other resources for people to explore:

Never Pray Again – coming soon from Chalice Press

Favorite quotes:

Many that live deserve death. And some that die deserve life. Can you give it to them? Then do not be too eager to deal out death in judgment. For even the very wise cannot see all ends.

—Gandalf

Christianity is a religion that critiques religion.

—Peter Rollins

I aim to misbehave.

—Malcolm Reynolds

If you want to tell people the truth, make them laugh, otherwise they'll kill you.
—Oscar Wilde

One chief cause of the amount of unbelief in the world is, that those who have seen something of the glory of Christ, set themselves to theorize concerning him rather than to obey him.

—George MacDonald

Five things people can do today, in their own community, to help make the world a better place:

1. Play. Take joy in this world and this life and add joy to other people's lives.

2. Stop praying. Don't wait for a supernatural force to intervene. Get out there and make a difference directly.
3. Stop defending God. God doesn't need your help. Instead, defend those weaker (poorer, less privileged, etc.) than yourself.
4. Make things. You are not a consumer; you are a creator. Act like it.
5. Support creativity. Encourage people you know to make things. Get on Kickstarter and help people who make things. Spread the joy of creating stuff.